MEANWHILE I KEEP DANCING

Tamsin Coates

Action Deafness Books
The Peepul Centre
Leicester LE4 6DP
Email: adbooks@actiondeafnessbooks.co.uk
Website: www.actiondeafnessbooks.co.uk

Published by Action Deafness Books 2012

Cover designed by Euan Carter (www.euancarter.com)

Original front cover photograph by Sally Kate

ISBN 978 0 9570822 5 0

British Library Cataloguing-in-Publication Data. A catalogue record for this book is available from the British Library.

Printed in the UK by Henry Ling, Dorchester, Dorset

Contents

List of Photographs

In colour section

Other resources

Acknowledgements

At the risk of becoming an Oscar acceptance style litany of names, there are several people I would like, and need, to thank.

Firstly thanks to Lauren Metcalfe and everyone at Action Deafness Books for believing that my story would have value in re-telling for other families and helping it come to fruition. Also thank you to my editor Amy L. Scott (http://www.nomadeditorial.com) for making this my words, story and voice but 'better'!

There have been so many professionals, from varied specialities, who have been involved with the boys over the years that it would be impossible to name them all individually. I am grateful for the care, time and consideration which everyone has shown them. I do have to mention special thanks to Anna Bradley, Bridget McNally, Emma Mottram and Greer Lacey who were there at the start and who provided so much help and guidance in laying the foundations for what the boys have achieved to date. Thank you, I seriously don't think we would be where we are now without you.

My sanity and sense of humour I owe to my friends and family. Many of my friends are parents of deaf or hearing impaired children themselves. To all those whose story I have shared here, thank you. To all of you and your children, thank you for being part of our lives- to have people who know your life and it's pressures, without needing to hear the words said, is an irreplaceable support network for me now and will be for the boys always.

Thank you to all my other friends with whom I have engaged in madcap activities over the years, from running to socialising and comedy nights you have all played an important part. I also want to thank those people who have been part of my life but aren't now. I hold all my memories dear to me and know how much you have helped me, not only practically, but also to have faith in the person I am and to become the woman and mother I am.

Lastly I must thank those people without whom this list would not be complete. The reasons I need to thank these people are too many and numerous to list but, suffice to say, I could not function as I do without them.

So a huge thank-you to Janine and Tony Probbing and Lisa 'Cici Fallenstar' Heenan and their amazing children Adam and Caitlin & Ben, Charlie and Isla whom I adore and who my children think of as family.

To all of my family; my parents, Rosemary and Paul, step parents, Robert and

Sharron, my brother John and not forgetting 'Auntie Sue', thank you for all you have done to encourage me over the years. This writing ability is all down to you. Thank you for all the proof reading and support. Also thank you to my parents-in law, Iris and Les, for their support in this process and special thanks to Iris for the artist's representation of a cochlear implant.

Lastly, to my husband Matt and my children Cameron, Campbell and Emma: you provide me with the sunshine moments which make me laugh and carry on regardless- even when you are driving me potty! This book was written for several reasons, but amongst them was a need I felt to document for the boys their story. So as they grow and mature they can look back at decisions and choices which have been made and perhaps understand them a little better. I am so proud of each of my children for their unique strengths, talents and abilities to make me smile or laugh out loud, even when I'm feeling blue. So a huge thank you to my little family; I love you all.

Preface

I get up. I walk. I fall down. Meanwhile I keep dancing.
– Hillel

This is my story, yet it is not my story alone. This is the story of a journey many people travel along, a path with many twists and turns and very few signposts. There are times when we can take a moment to admire a miracle of nature with someone close; from a resting spot we stop and drink in the amazing view or relish a soothing sunset. In between these moments there are ravines to traverse and arduous climbs where we seem to never reach the top. There are blisters, bumps, and bruises that need tending and an all-consuming exhaustion we must fight through. It is a journey with no shortcuts but numerous crossroads where decisions need to be made about which direction to go. It will take a lifetime to complete.

This book is a travel journal of my journey so far; it's also a guidebook to help other parents who embark on a new path from the time they find out their child is deaf. Many of the experiences described here are not unique to families with a deaf child, though; they may also resonate and sound familiar to families whose children have other diagnoses or difficulties. When I was expecting my first son, this was not the journey I had anticipated or prepared myself for. I had read baby books, seen friends with their children, and combined all that with media images to imagine how family life would be. But so much of the terrain we have covered so far has been unexpected territory for us as a family and for me as a parent; it wasn't on that original map or itinerary I had in my head.

In this book I describe some of the major gateways I have passed through so far. Along the way I have learned of many different opinions and points of view, but the most important thing I have learned is that despite the difficulties we may encounter as parents, we have to relax and appreciate these new surroundings, and we have to enjoy every silly moment we can with our children.

At times my family's trail has crossed paths with someone else's, and we've had company along the way. I share some of their stories in this book. Sometimes our companions have been there for only a mile or two, or have helped us around a particular obstacle. Others have stayed for a seeming marathon distance. With them we shared what we had learned on our journey so far, and we also gained from their knowledge and experiences. We swapped anecdotes and shared the joy of success with each stride (or small step) taken. We laughed, cried, and grew together. At some point their path took a different direction from ours, and we moved on, treasuring our memories of the time we travelled together. There are also those who are with us for the duration of our journey in one way or another – those people in our lives who know us so well, who know our strengths and skills, our weaknesses and flaws, and who love, support, and protect us because of (and despite) them. These companions provide essential nourishment as I travel this path, and they have known when to walk next to me and when to fall back and let me walk alone for a while.

This journey begins with the arrival of a child, from that first moment when we hold that tiny (or not so tiny!) bundle in our arms and realize this being depends upon us completely. As our little ones grow and reach towards the big wide world, they need us beside them to hold their hands, to teach them, to stretch them, and to fight for them. These are common duties for all parents, but some of us need to be there a bit longer, supporting our children as they reach milestones and find their way to independence on their own timeline. Children who are deaf or have other special needs may need some extra time and carefully constructed scaffolding to help them reach the edge of the nest and fly free. Parents tend to remember when their children achieved each 'first', such as when they first spoke. I waited a long time for my sons to reach that milestone, but I also got to celebrate so many other little milestones along the way. Each was a small reward for the effort it took for me to walk and sustain forward momentum through the often-difficult periods on this path.

My hope is that this book can be a companion to any parent or carer on this journey or on a parallel path, whether just starting out or already several miles further on. It can be picked up, put down, and revisited in the future as needed. Like sharing a big mug of tea and a box of tissues with a friend. It offers comfort as well as a reminder that you are not alone – even though it may feel like it at times. Like any travel guide, it provides relevant history, shares other traveller's views and experiences, and highlights those moments that shouldn't be missed despite other distractions. Within these pages I hope you will find validation for your feelings about the struggles you face and the triumphs you achieve. I want to reassure you that they are reasonable and that others are having the same feelings and going through similar situations.

My other hope is that not only parents will pick up this book, but also professionals and other people who have not travelled this path as we have. This book can only give snapshot glimpses into our world, but those snapshots will give readers some true insight into our thoughts and internal struggles, as we try to take the most rational and effective steps we can in bringing up our children.

Grief and Acceptance

Cares are often more difficult to throw off than sorrows,
the latter die with time, the former grow.

– Jean Paul

However mean your life is, meet it and live it.

– Henry David Thoreau

As a young girl, I was a typical 'little mother'. I loved caring for my dolls, dressing them, and pretending they were dependant on me. One Christmas I was given a blue gingham cloth apron by a distant relative. Many other girls would have thrown it away in disgust, but I wore it with pride. It made me feel like Ma Walton standing out on her porch watching her brood. Goodness knows what the neighbours thought of me! As I grew older and moved on to Barbie dolls, I made sure they all had huge families. My Barbie and Ken would typically have twins followed by triplets, and their brood would grow and grow.

An instinctive part of me always craved a large family. This was in direct contrast to my own family, which was small. My parents were both only children, so my brother and I had no cousins, aunts, or uncles. With long distances separating us from both sets of grandparents, we were quite a small, self-contained family unit. I was twelve when my parents separated and later divorced. Although they both subsequently remarried, neither of them had any more children, and I still wanted to be part of a large extended family like those I saw on television.

During my school years I was always slightly socially awkward, always on the fringes of the group. I was included but was not at the centre of the action. Unsure of myself, I observed those more naturally adept. I joined the Duke of Edinburgh Award Scheme offered by our school and followed where it took me. This scheme offered challenges and opportunities to find direction in those middle teenage years which could have otherwise left me aimless. I was encouraged to fulfil commitments to learn new skills, help in my local community, and take part in group outdoor expeditions. These expeditions took place in all kinds of conditions, from knee-deep snow to glorious sunshine, and through each I found new depths of both self-reliance and cooperation with others. The satisfaction that we found in reaching our campsite, when only hours before we had thought we were hopelessly lost, usurped the panic we had felt. Through those adventures

I began to learn about and grow into myself as an individual. In our last year of school our group travelled to Spain for our final challenge within the Duke of Edinburgh scheme. Half of the group opted to travel by plane and the rest of us chose to travel by minibus. Our convoluted journey from Scotland went through England across to France and ended in the Pyrenees in the north of Spain. By the time we met up with our friends who had travelled by plane, we had so much to tell and share. Instead of handing over our bags, getting on a plane, sitting for a couple of hours, and then going through baggage claim, we had had quite the adventure: being confined to our tents during thunderstorms in France and finding amusement in travel pillows and fashionable ways to wear them; or enjoying group meals where we all shared giant tins of sausages and beans that we found in a French supermarket, scooped out with pieces of fresh baguette.

In that minibus I learned so much. I learned about the joy and memories that are made in spontaneous shared moments and recognised the enjoyment found in each small step of our journey. We had experienced discomfort and had general cabin fever from being in a small confined space for days on end, yet none of us would have swapped our travel plans for the other group's seemingly easier route. We had ended up in the same place, but to those of us who had travelled the long way, our journey was the preferable one. Little did I know the foundations this was laying down for my life ahead and how valuable that lesson would be.

I went on to college, where I met my future husband. We were both studying degrees to become health professionals: Lee to become an Occupational Therapist, and I to become a Speech and Language Therapist. I enjoyed my course and the placements I completed as part of the course requirements. Some placements were with adults, and I found the work to be both interesting and satisfying, but there was never any doubt in my mind that I wanted to be in paediatrics, to work with children who had difficulties with communication and to support their families. Lee and I married young, before I had even completed the last year of my four-year course. Lee came from a broken family background and had spent time in boarding school while his parents travelled with the armed forces. He wanted that secure family base of his own that he never had. I felt perfectly matched to him because all I had wanted since I was tiny was to have children of my own to care for. Our wedding was a happy occasion, a perfect day with all our friends and relatives around us. It was exciting to be creating our own family unit.

Shortly after we married we moved nearly 200 miles, from Edinburgh to Merseyside. It was a huge move away from all that was familiar. It took us from the capital city of Scotland to the northwest of England, from a city that bustled with tourists all year round and echoed with the sound of pipers playing bagpipes on street corners during the summer months, to the Wirral peninsula where countryside is never more than a ten-minute drive away. It was a decision we made together, though, as the best option for us both starting out in our careers. Lee had some relatives in the area, and friends from college also lived nearby. After a couple of years the time felt right to try for a family. I initially became pregnant over the millennium. We started this new era with joyous news that couldn't have come at a more opportune time for our families. Over that Christmas and New Year period Lee's family had been involved in a car crash with devastating effects, and my stepfather had suffered a severe stroke out of the blue. Our news gave everyone something positive to focus on, so we told them very early on. In truth, we also couldn't contain our excitement.

Sadly, I miscarried before I reached the twelve-week mark. I was devastated. It had never entered my head when I set out into pregnancy that anything could go wrong. Miscarriage at that time was still not often discussed or publicised for fear of frightening people. I felt like it was not something I should need to discuss with people beyond the obvious initial sympathies, which were followed by awkwardness and a swift move to change the topic. But for me it was a difficult time and inside I was heartbroken. The moment I had seen the positive result of the pregnancy test, I had skipped ahead mentally to the baby I would hold in my arms and push in a pram. To me it was all very real, and the loss hurt. For the benefit of other people I struggled to pretend that nothing had happened, but I needed to acknowledge my feelings and give them a voice. I couldn't quite find a way to do that at the time, though, and I continued to carry the sorrow and apprehension I was left with. Over time, I encountered others who had similar experiences, and through talking with them I could finally release the pent-up emotion in a safe and shared narrative. To this day I still remember the date the baby was due, and that child holds a special place in my heart.

After a time, Lee and I recognised that although we could not replace the baby we had lost, we were still desperate to start our family. So we tried again, this time with more nerves and awareness that things could go wrong. We had also talked about the difficulties children can have and how we would feel about that, having learned first-hand that not everything always goes as smoothly as we initially expect. Our eyes had been opened, and because I worked with children who not only had communication difficulties, but also physical difficulties, learning difficulties, and a variety of different syndromes, it was a very real possibility to me that our child could have a difficulty of some description. I knew that having a child with difficulties would not matter to me, but I needed to discuss it with Lee. He seemed confident that we could cope together with any challenge that arose, so in a relatively short space of time I became pregnant again.

This time I felt as if I were walking on eggshells through the whole of the first trimester, expecting that something could go wrong at every turn. But my pregnancy progressed normally and I worked through to my maternity leave. Our son Cameron was born early when I began to experience problems at the end of my pregnancy. He arrived to such joy and relief: our family life had started. Cameron was a happy baby, calm and sociable. He was a joy to look after and smiled at everyone he met. When Cameron was about six months old, we found out that I was pregnant again – it had not been a conscious decision, but it was not unwelcome news nonetheless. We would have two children under two years old, and, as everyone was at pains to point out, we'd have our work cut out for us!

At around the same time we learned of my pregnancy, we went away on holiday to Cornwall with some of Lee's family. Cameron had up to this point been hitting all his developmental milestones and would babble away to people who stopped to speak to him on trips to the supermarket. I glowed with maternal pride every time anyone commented on how chatty he was. Our journey to Cornwall took us a good six hours, and during that time spent confined in the car with our gorgeous son, we realised that he hadn't babbled at all the whole way. Instead he made a noise, sucking air in, that made it sound like he was having trouble breathing. Having stopped a couple of times to check that he was OK and not in great distress, we started to discuss when we'd last heard him babbling and where this sound had come from. We realised that during the past week those trademark gurgles and sounds that were part of Cameron's sociable persona had been absent. As our week's holiday progressed, this breathing noise seemed to have stuck and the babbling didn't return.

We returned home and began to observe more and more things that caused concern. When we were at a friend's house preparing for a birthday party, balloons started to burst because of the friction of them rubbing together in the crammed kitchen. My friend and I were jumping out of our seats as balloon after balloon burst with a loud bang, but Cameron sat unaffected, grinning away, and did not flinch at the loud noises. The following week I phoned our health visitor and asked for a referral for a hearing test. I told her that something wasn't right; knowing my profession, she agreed to refer us directly through for a hearing test.

Cameron was seen for assessment, and the doctors agreed that he seemed to be having a little bit of trouble with his hearing and that his communication was behind. They believed that glue ear was causing the problem and explained that it could be resolved with a simple procedure to insert grommets, or small plastic tubes, into the eardrums. At this point I was heavily pregnant and unsure of myself. I phoned my work and asked to speak to our hearing specialist. She tried to reassure me that glue ear could cause a substantial loss, but when she heard the doubt in my voice I think she knew that as a mum I intuitively knew that there was something more.

Whilst waiting for Cameron's operation to treat the glue ear, I was preparing for the imminent arrival of our second child. Another boy – we would have two little boys who would grow up to play cops and robbers together. Despite anticipating the inevitable hard work and exhaustion that was to come, my excitement at wanting to see my new son and have my two boys together was building. At my final pre-natal appointments I asked if it would be possible for the baby to have Newborn Hearing Screening, which at that time was not offered to every newborn baby as it is now. Call it instinct, but I wanted my baby checked. Lee's family thought I was overestimating Cameron's difficulties. Why would I imagine that the baby would have any difficulty at all?

Campbell arrived early like his brother and for the same reasons. He was a sturdy baby with rugby player's shoulders who liked his milk and loved his mum. He was only truly settled when he was nestled against me. Campbell was the opposite of Cameron; he didn't like being handed to anyone else. His first hearing test showed problems, but I was reassured that it may have been the result of fluid from the birth that remained in his ear canals. Campbell was then retested in the same week as Cameron's grommet operation. First, Campbell failed his retest. Then Cameron had his operation. When the surgeon did his ward round and asked if we had seen any difference in Cameron since he had awoken from his anaesthetic and I had to admit 'no' – there was no change, an alarm bell tolled. The next day I phoned my health visitor again. This time I'm sure I sounded like a madwoman, manic and demanding my boys be seen for further assessment. And properly this time – were people not aware of the circumstances unfolding? I needed this dealt with. Waiting felt futile; we had been in limbo and now needed answers.

Diagnosis, when it comes, is a different experience for every family. To start, the causes of hearing loss or impairment are many and varied. For some families diagnosis follows an acute episode in hospital with their child. Perhaps their child has suffered a head injury or illness such as meningitis or measles. The family has watched the child in medical distress and perhaps even fighting for life. When a diagnosis of a subsequent hearing difficulty is determined, they are torn. Parents are understandably thankful that their child is still with them and recovering, but they are concerned about this new aspect to comprehend and accommodate. For other families the diagnosis of hearing difficulties may be part of a larger picture. For example, with premature babies, small and vulnerable, hearing difficulties may be secondary to other more pressing issues involved in their care. The child's age at diagnosis can also affect how families react. When a child is diagnosed at a later age, the family may feel frustrated to see how much time has passed and seemingly been wasted without knowing what was affecting their child. With younger children diagnosed very soon after birth, the parents' process of bonding with and getting to know their new baby can be complicated by the diagnosis.

We took Cameron and Campbell for the appointment which would shake our world when Campbell was three months and Cameron eighteen months. Looking back it was almost slapstick in organisation. For this hearing test the boys needed to be asleep, and it was decided that they would not give Campbell a sedative but instead would test him while he was just naturally asleep. But he didn't want to 'play ball' and, probably sensing our tension, was having a fractious afternoon. After we had struggled for a while, I ended up breast-feeding him to calm him whilst one of the audiologists held the headphone to his ear – there was no room for dignity at this point. Once they had measured Campbell's brain response to the noises, it was time to swap. Lee took Campbell out and it was Cameron's turn. Cameron had been given the sedative earlier, but while he was sleeping his forehead had become sweaty. They needed to wipe his forehead clean to attach the electrodes, and as they did so he woke up. We then had to try to get him back to sleep, so we walked what seemed like miles up and down the hospital corridor with him in a buggy until he dropped off. We were relieved once Cameron's assessment was complete; the process had been draining. But we still had to re-enter the room to hear the results: both our boys were deaf.

As we sat there, words washed around us. The boys would need further testing over the coming months to more accurately assess their levels of deafness. They were both affected in their left and right ears and would need to start wearing two hearing aids as soon as possible. To that end, they needed to take ear impressions while we were there that day so they could make the moulds. Words, information, and details all flowed past me as I looked at my children and thought about what this meant. Prior to this appointment I had almost accepted, in my heart of hearts, that Cameron would be given this diagnosis. We had seen the signs and started our journey with him. Yet looking down at Campbell, my baby, asleep in my arms – how could they be telling me something so huge about him?

My thoughts were divided. My two boys would always have each other, a sibling close in age who was taking a similar path. They would have someone to turn to who knew their experiences and challenges, and they could grow together. We weren't facing a life where they would be compared against each other, deaf versus hearing. But then I felt guilt and sorrow for thinking this way. While rationalising that it was good for Cameron to have a brother who was also deaf, we were facing devastating news about this little bundle who had only been with us for a couple of months. We hadn't yet had the opportunity to learn his quirks –

what made him laugh, what food he would spit out – in the natural way of things as we had with Cameron. We now faced the reality of bringing Campbell up in a very different way.

Numb, we made our way home. Our journey with our boys had just taken a swift move off the path we had assumed we would follow and down a previously unnoticed slip road. We would have to learn to steer fast to maintain control. There was little real time to process our feelings. We still had two children under age two who needed to be cared for, and we needed to share this news with our families and those closest to us. Within two weeks both boys had two hearing aids each and we had to take in all the relevant information quickly. We had to mitigate the danger of our babies' ready access to batteries, which are harmful if swallowed. There was a seemingly constant threat of the loss of the hearing aids out of the buggy, frequent re-moulds, and troubleshooting with the equipment to take on board. In addition we welcomed a whole new host of people into our lives, including all the necessary professionals: teachers of the deaf, teaching assistants, speech and language therapists, community paediatricians, and audiologists, to name but a few. All these people needed to be consulted with and given feedback, and we had to take advice from and agree targets with them.

Soon after diagnosis, our audiologist referred us on to a paediatrician. The boys would need various medical assessments on their hearts, kidneys, and eyes to check how they were functioning. In cases where there is no family history of hearing loss or deafness, they need to check for abnormalities to rule out syndromes that could be linked to the hearing diagnosis. Those first few weeks and months post-diagnosis passed in a whirl. I still have my wall calendar from that year, each day's plans written in tiny cramped writing to fit it all in, with extra notes and numbers scrawled on any available blank spaces, a testament to our daily visitors, appointments, and check-ups.

The news about the initial diagnosis became dwarfed by worry about other potential complications, such as the possibility that they could also go blind over the next couple of years. I couldn't begin to fathom the concept that, having already lost one sense, my boys could also lose their sight. My fear that this would be the case nearly paralysed me. For several days I let the fear overwhelm me and could barely function for the thoughts running through my head. This worry eventually taught me a valuable lesson. After a time I realised that I could give in to this fear, and all the others, but how would that help? Instead, I could face one day at a time and accomplish within it as much as I could – but to do this I could not 'borrow' trouble. I could not live life assuming that these things would happen. I had to believe that we would deal with each thing as it occurred. We would learn to roll with each punch and then get up and move forward again.

Eventually we found out the cause of their deafness and associated thyroid difficulties. Their hearing loss is caused by a genetic syndrome called Pendred Syndrome that occurred because their dad and I each carried specific genes. Pendred Syndrome can affect people's hearing to varying degrees but it is generally a progressive hearing loss, in which residual hearing can deteriorate over time. We were lucky to have a name for the cause of the boys' difficulties, as often there is no conclusive answer. But it took time; these answers did not come until the boys were seven and eight years old – more than six years after the investigations began. Learning to look past my fears saved us spending all that time in limbo.

Over time we adapted to our new lives. I slipped relatively easily into coping mode, never sitting down and fully acknowledging the depth of my grief for the boys and the turn our lives had taken. Even in writing this I am still experiencing and dealing with the emotion I stored up. I didn't have time for tears then, and somehow I didn't need them on a day-to-day basis. They were still my boys, my babies, and they were cheeky little monkeys to boot! Of course there were moments that made me stop, when a thought would come to me or I would become aware of a lump in my throat. I'd remember small things such as how stupidly proud I had been that I had 'trained' Cameron from a young age to sleep whilst I would vacuum around him. Well, of course he could sleep through that; he hadn't been able to hear it, and I hadn't realised. To move forward, however, I could not dwell in the past and feel regret. I had to accept where we were now and help my children develop, grow, and fulfil their potential. I would do whatever needed to be done for them, whatever best met their needs, and whilst doing all that I would try my hardest to enjoy every minute with them without suffocating them.

In some ways, we were lucky that Cameron had been diagnosed late. Campbell was receiving earlier intervention, and over time this could positively affect his progress and outcome, but having had no diagnosis for Cameron for over a year we had brought him up in the rough-and-tumble laughter-filled and unfettered way we had always envisaged we would, the same way our friends were raising their children. We had not felt that need to overly protect or shelter him that a diagnosis often provokes, that desire to wrap our children up in cotton wool and not let them out of our sight, and a need to second-guess every decision we make for them. Instead, I had a toddler who loved nothing more than being looked after by my friend and playing with her children. He was at ease being taken to new places and seeing new things, especially if it involved fish or motorbikes! Life with Cameron pre-diagnosis had set the tone for how we would continue. Our boys may have needed extra consideration at times, but we needed them to grow up with other children around them, doing the same things and living life to the full. Every time they smiled for a camera while taking part in some activity with their friends, oblivious to any differences, it reinforced that we were on the right track for the time being.

As one would imagine, the reactions we got from the people around us differed. Those people closest to us were able to listen and offer practical help where they could. For others it must have been more difficult, and we saw that in the way they related to us and expressed their feelings about our situation. Sometimes this was hurtful and invoked our defensiveness. I remember clearly a comment made by a family member about a photo of Cameron I had sent. She had phoned to thank me and tell me what a lovely photo it was, but what a shame you could see his hearing aid in it. I was stunned. Over time I had stopped noticing the presence of the hearing aids when I looked at the boys; the devices were part of them. Anger rose up. It was a picture of my son and his hearing aids were not optional; they were a necessity. Of course, the comment was not said to upset or incite me. It is only with time that I can look back and see that in her way that person felt helpless; she was observing what had happened in our lives but could not fix it or make it go away. She cared about us but didn't know what to say and could not offer a solution, so she had tried her best.

Other people appeared indifferent to the multiple balls we were metaphorically juggling, our way of life, and what we needed to prioritise. They seemed to ignore what was occurring and show no consideration for it. Again, with time and a more experienced view, I have realised that some people can't sympathise, beyond polite enquiry, when they have no experience or knowledge of what someone is going through. To truly understand they would have to actively live our life and walk a mile in our shoes. Each person has their own raw spots and sorrow, and most people do not want more. For some, it is easier to pretend others' problems don't exist.

It is not only in reactions from outside the family that we find differences. Any diagnosis for our child, including hearing impairment or deafness, is a huge stress for parents. How we feel, react, accept, and move forward can differ hugely from how our partner or spouse will handle the situation. As with all difficulties shared by a couple, a diagnosis can bring them closer together, confirming unity and shared direction. For other couples, a chasm can appear between them as differing understandings or views cause disagreement on major decisions.

Often one parent takes the role of primary caregiver and assumes the weight of responsibility for attending appointments, working on targets, chasing up responses or reports, and managing the plethora of daily tasks that go hand in hand with raising children. This can arise by choice or circumstance. In some families where one parent works away, or in single-parent families, this is a necessity. In other homes it can come about due to the partners' differing levels of acceptance of the situation. While one parent is able to accept the diagnosis, move forward, and make steps to prepare for the long journey ahead, the other parent struggles. It is easier for this other parent to seemingly avoid learning about the situation, to purposefully ignore its existence and continue his or her role in family life unchanged, whilst his or her partner takes the lead in meeting the new needs which have quickly become integral to daily life.

Some couples can successfully navigate this in an intricate balance that somehow makes the relationship whole. Other couples find it more of a challenge to adjust their partnership. When one parent has the majority of the responsibility, the burden can be heavy. That parent alone may be deemed responsible, by him or herself and by the other parent, for choosing a path, making decisions, and moving forward. Resentments can build as one parent takes ownership of the situation and feels isolated or abandoned by the other parent, who seems to benefit from being detached from the situation.

In our family, I held the responsibility for attending appointments, communicating with professionals, and working towards targets with the children. That was how our situation worked out, and whilst I would not have swapped my role or abdicated the care of my children to anyone else, at times I felt the strain.

Through this role, I was facing the daily reality of what the boys' diagnosis meant for them as individuals and for us as a family. Having to face that reality so blatantly is a double-edged sword. I was the parent who at the end of a long day with my children sometimes looked at what we had done and realised how little time had been spent on introducing new sounds, developing language or in purposeful play. If their communication didn't progress, would I regret, and alone be responsible for, those lost hours? In appointments I could be asked so many questions about their development or the involvement of other professionals. I would feel strongly that I needed to access from my memory all the information being requested, or the person we were consulting with would not have the complete picture. This could make a difference in an intervention being successful or not. I could share so many examples of how the pressure and weight of responsibility subtly and instinctively grew for me. On the other side, however, in facing what this diagnosis meant for the boys, I was also facing directly who our little boys were and I was accepting our situation. Whilst I would have preferred for them not to have these challenges in life, I could see they were developing in skills and character regardless. I was building my faith in their future from seeing their mischief and mishaps every day. In that regard, I felt disconnected from their father.

It is human nature to want to try to escape when things are not as we expect or are difficult. By being distracted, often subconsciously, one can take a break from what needs to be addressed. There is a comfort in being lost in other thoughts or being 'too busy', but it hinders acceptance and, in my experience, the ability to share the load with the other parent.

The hardest part of holding the majority of responsibility, I found, came when I had to face bad news in appointments, such as diagnosis, awareness of deterioration, new areas for concern, and the need for further tests, to name but a few. Almost always, I was the only one there in that moment; I was the one who needed to be strong. In the face of devastating news, often delivered by a stranger, I would fight to keep my composure. Inside I was shaking and crumbling from the blow, but I needed to form sentences to gain further information or respond. Plus, I needed to care for my children while the professionals gave often-long explanations, and then we had to find our way home. In those moments I felt most keenly the need for a person, my partner, beside me to prop me up and diffuse the intensity of feeling between the two of us instead of it weighing on just one. To share the need to focus and remember to ask those pertinent questions that can so easily slip your mind when you are alone.

Being the person carrying most of the responsibility is such a unique position to be in, and I know that at the time I felt that my level of involvement and the pressure I felt was miles away from what I believed my husband felt.

It is similar to one's perception of an object's size at different distances. From afar, the scope of what needs to be dealt with can appear small; however, when one moves closer, it becomes larger and more overwhelming. If we stand so near that our vision becomes fuzzy, then our perception of what we face becomes distorted and out of proportion. Finding the distance that gives us the most accurate view can be difficult; we need to rely on others to remind us to take a small step back when we are too close. We also must encourage others to move closer, to share the view we have and see the size of the problem from our perspective. But just as importantly, we want them to stand with us and look beyond the problem to enjoy the central focus, the child, together.

Coming to terms with my children's diagnosis and its implications has not been a finite event, or the completion of a single episode. Over time, just as the tide ebbs and flows, different aspects of how this diagnosis will affect my children have come to the fore at pertinent times. As issues are resolved they drift away from my immediate consciousness. Then, after a spell of calm, the waves will bring something new to the surface. Many of these challenges awaken the feelings I have been through before, and at times they have made me acknowledge all over again the direction life has taken us and the path we now follow.

Most people would probably prefer a life they can anticipate, that has elements of stability and predictability. We are shaped to desire familiarity. But as parents we must face the ways in which our journeys will shift over time. We cannot be static. The landscape around us will change with every step we take and new landmarks will come into sight. Getting accustomed to the uncertainty that each new junction in the road will bring can help us remain steadfast as we consider, 'Where to next?'

Decisions

Do what you can, with what you have, where you are.
Theodore Roosevelt

When Campbell was nine months old, we approached a major crossroads, not knowing as it appeared on the horizon that this junction would change and define the coming years. Both boys, in the early stages of their diagnosis, had to go for regular appointments with audiology to get new moulds and to have hearing assessments performed to check how, and what, they could hear with their hearing aids. The moulds were tiny and needed to be remade every few weeks to accommodate the boys' growth. At this particular appointment Campbell's hearing was to be checked, and our doctor was very interested to know whether we had observed Campbell turning to noises he might have heard. At the end of the appointment he was able to tell me that Campbell's hearing had deteriorated. Even with hearing aids he was not hearing sounds well, and he would not be able to hear the sounds of the words we were saying to him. He told me that we must be referred to Manchester University for assessment by a different team, where we would face a new decision: whether, if Campbell were found to be an appropriate candidate, to accept a cochlear implant for our son.

This crossroads is one that doesn't appear on every journey, but when it does appear, it's a BIG one! There are signposts with lots of directions encouraging us to both paths. But the paths go in opposite directions, which makes it a difficult place for parents to choose which way to lead their children. One path is very well travelled, and whilst it's new to us, it has a whole community waiting to stand by our side and help us along. It is a path that perhaps has more restrictions along the way, but it does not have medical uncertainty for life. It is also a path that for some may have regrets or 'what ifs' further down the road. The other path seems fairly new and less well trod, but it looks appealing and promises so much. Once we step onto it, however, we must prepare for a roller-coaster ride that will match the biggest a theme park has to offer, with highs, lows, and lots of holding on and closing our eyes and wishing we could put the brakes on for just a minute to catch our breath. So which way to go?

Cochlear implants are relatively unknown to most people. Not many people have them, and hearing people often mistake cochlear implants for hearing aids, probably because the external part of the cochlear implant is worn on the ear in the same way as a hearing aid. Some implants have power packs attached which are worn in a harness or pinned to clothing. The cochlear implant also has a component which is surgically implanted in the ear; it contains a magnet which attracts the magnet of the external piece to hold it in place.

Cochlear implants are only suitable for some deaf people. A child's or adult's level of hearing loss is usually a good initial indicator to determine whether implants are suitable. Levels of hearing loss are sometimes described in percentages, but this is not accurate; hearing loss is measured in decibels (dBs). Based on the decibel levels that a person can hear, his or her level of deafness is described as mild, moderate, severe, or profound. For example, a child may be described as having a loss of eighty decibels, which means he cannot detect sounds below eighty decibels and can only just hear eighty-decibel sounds. Typically, a person with normal hearing can hear sound at ten to fifteen decibels; eighty decibels is roughly the volume of someone shouting loudly. This child's results would be described as being in the 'severe' range of hearing loss.

Hearing aids help people hear by making sounds louder. Often, making the sounds louder is enough to enable children and adults with mild to severe hearing loss to hear them. For other children and adults with severe to profound hearing loss, however, this is not sufficient to help them hear. They may have absent or damaged hair cells from any of a variety of causes. For them to hear, their hearing nerve must be stimulated directly, bypassing the hair cells. With a cochlear implant, sound goes into the microphone on the external piece and is then converted into a special signal which is transmitted as an electrical message. This message travels from the speech processor directly to the hearing nerve via electrodes which have been surgically placed in the cochlea, and sound is then heard by the brain as a signal which it learns to recognise.

For those who would like to know more, I have included more detail, diagrams, and charts describing levels of hearing loss and cochlear implants at the end of this book in the section titled 'Further Information'.

On his last assessment, the audiologist had found that Campbell's hearing had dropped from the severe to the profound level of deafness. For some sounds tested he did not even respond to noises made at 100 dBs, equivalent to the noise level of a helicopter in flight. The referral to evaluate whether different technology would be beneficial for him was appropriate. Campbell was first seen at the Cochlear Implant Centre in Manchester on the day after his first birthday, and the assessment process began.

A cochlear implant is considered standard treatment for profound deafness in children (and some adults) who are assessed as appropriate candidates. Those recommending it to parents as an option for their child see it as a no-brainer, a technological breakthrough that has transformed the lives of people who have had the procedure (with individual degrees of success, but most will gain some benefit). Offering the choice of a cochlear implant to a deaf person has been compared, by those supportive of this procedure, to recommending glasses to someone who has vision difficulties or providing a daily living aid device for those with mobility problems. Supporters view cochlear implants as a logical, effective, and appropriate solution.

We left the appointment in Manchester with lots on our minds but confident of a possible direction we could go. We were dealing with the need to accept our child's level of hearing loss as well as the grief that comes with it – accepting the reality that there were limited options that might lead to him being able to hear and, indeed, wondering whether he ever would. For a parent, these are huge emotions that naturally lead to worries about the near future, as well as five years in the future, when the child goes to high school, then college, and forms friendships, relationships, starts a family and so on. There are many other areas that could be added to this list, and I know my female brain can take that worrying to a whole new level (or so I'm told! Thank you, hubby dear), but I know I'm not alone. Being offered a life line, a very real way to try and change this for my child, is appealing, but it's also scary – it involves head surgery, there are possible risks. But it's an option worth mulling over and formulating questions about.

I didn't know other families who had gone through the same decision process, so Google was a logical place to go for information. However, doing a search on cochlear implants brought a huge reality check about what we were contemplating. Words like 'unnecessary', 'oppressive', and 'potentially harmful' leapt off the screen and challenged all that we had been thinking.

I learned that for the Deaf Community, the arrival of the cochlear implant has ignited a lot of feeling. They embrace their identity as Deaf people, and they affirm that their Deafness is an acceptable alternative to hearing. It is widely reported that the Deaf Community feel Deafness should be looked at as an element of cultural diversity, not a disability, and not something that needs to be 'fixed' or 'repaired'. In addition, there is the implication that society on the whole must learn to accept and understand differences and that deaf children should be proud of who they are and not ashamed of what they are born with. Some people in the Deaf Community feel that the decision to have a cochlear implant indicates that one is ashamed of being deaf, or that parents who make the decision for their child are ashamed of their child being deaf.

My personal values wholeheartedly support these statements, and these ideas provoked much deliberation and second-guessing for me. It was difficult to acknowledge that I, as a parent, was actually considering this procedure for my child.

We needed to review the benefits, risks, and long-term implications again in light of these opinions. We were contemplating head surgery that would open up a pathway to the brain. The surgery carries risks from the anaesthetic and possible side effects such as facial nerve damage. In implanting the components the surgeons would destroy any residual hearing in that ear, and at that time they were only fourteen years on from the first cochlear implant surgery. There was no way of predicting what the implications of having the implant were over the course of a normal life span. Add to this that by agreeing to the procedure, I could be conveying to my child that I think he is 'broken' and needs to be 'fixed'. Without the implant, my baby could grow up as a healthy boy who used signing to communicate, had a supportive family, and never knew any different than his own experience to date. The no-brainer proposition was quickly becoming a conundrum.

For many parents, balancing out these negatives and fears is a very strong weight: the weight of parental responsibility and our desire for the most that is possible for our children. One friend of mine, who was musical all through her childhood, says the one thing that still causes her to pause and gives her a pang of regret for her two deaf children is that they will never hear music as she does. It is a weight that she carries but only acknowledges occasionally, for in every other way she brings up her children with compassion and not pity, with confidence and not fear. A cochlear implant, I thought, could mean that my son would be able to hear music, birds, motorbikes, noisy toys, and the sound of the tide coming in on the River Mersey at the bottom of our street. It was possible that one day Campbell would be able to hear those waves that had soothed me so many times.

Looking at Campbell's future realistically, I knew that he could already be picked out from his peers and would continue to be so as he grew up, whether he was wearing an implant on his head or not. His use of sign, his hearing aids, and his withdrawal from the world around him and attachment to me alone marked him as different from his peers. But this operation could multiply the choices he would have over his lifetime. He could develop spoken language and understand others' speech. He could learn the value and enjoyment that can be gleaned from interacting with all those in the world around him. Campbell would still be able to choose at a later date to remove the entire implant or just the external component and live his life in a silent world, without the technology, if that was what he wanted. However, the reverse was not true; we couldn't leave the decision to have the implant for him to make when he was older: in his case, the time span for the cochlear implant to be successful was limited. This decision for him and for his future could only be made now, by us. Therein lay the deciding factor for me. I felt that if I limited his options by not doing the implant, I would not be able to face my son as a teenager and answer the questions he would inevitably ask as to why we didn't give him this opportunity. For the answer I would have to give Campbell was fear, my fear. Fear that something could go wrong and I could lose him or make his situation worse. Fear that the operation wouldn't work or that eventually he would resent the implant and reject it. I decided I had to find the strength to do this for him. I could not limit my child's opportunities.

I wanted the best of both worlds for my son. I wanted him to receive this medical treatment that promised so much. Yet I also still firmly believed that he should be raised to be proud of who he is, proud of his deaf identity and not ashamed of the condition he was born with. It is often felt that there is a divide between the Deaf Community and those who use cochlear implants, such as deaf children of hearing adults. This divide can lead to those with implants not fitting in socially with either the Deaf Community or the hearing world. I didn't want this for my child, obviously. However, I had to trust that as times were changing and this technology was becoming more prevalent, the Deaf Community would adjust to accommodate this new generation of deaf children. Attitudes towards disabilities are also changing within society in general. As a result of work and campaigning from many different groups representing people with disabilities, steps are being taken to create a more accepting society, with increased understanding of differences between people. The ideal situation will not happen overnight, but I hope it will appear within my lifetime. A tandem shift is required to both close the divide and also allow those with disabilities to feel less isolated and able to access all that these contrasting cultures can offer.

When we told our family and friends that we had decided to go ahead with the implant operation, they responded in quite a matter-of-fact way. To them it had been almost a foregone conclusion, a straightforward decision; they were unaware of the deeper conflict we had been wrestling with. Once the decision was made, one of the first reactions we encountered from the outside world was, by chance, from a deaf adult. She was a mature lady who taught the evening sign-language course we attended. One night I explained that I would probably miss the next session because we had an appointment in Manchester with Campbell and would not return in time. The tutor asked, in sign, what the appointment was for. I then endeavoured to explain using sign and ended up having to write key words on the blackboard, not having the breadth of sign vocabulary necessary for this conversation. Her response took few words, but it was emphatic: we were cruel, cruel for doing that to our child. I was at a loss for how to reply. Already plenty unsure of the decision we had made, and still unprepared to justify it to others, especially in sign, I walked away. I held myself together – just – and left. I knew these opinions existed, but had not expected them to be expressed so forcefully and judgementally to me by someone who knew comparatively little about our individual situation. The incident upset me greatly, but we stayed firm in our decision. I did not return to the signing course, though; I could not face that woman or her disapproval again, not at that stage in the process. To go through with this difficult decision, we had to put our heads down and push through. The emotional quandary the teacher had renewed in me could not be replayed weekly – it would weaken our resolve, and Campbell needed us to be strong.

Campbell's implant operation went ahead just after his second birthday. As I walked away from the operating theatre, looking back towards the big double doors behind which my son lay sedated and ready for surgery, my throat hurt from the lump of emotion stored there. I still questioned whether we had made the right decision. The operation itself went smoothly, but afterwards there were complications. The area around where the internal component had been inserted into Campbell's head was not healing as it should; there was internal bleeding in this area that the doctors had to stop – or risk the need to explant the whole device.

Campbell had to have subsequent surgeries over the following weeks, and we spent the majority of that stifling summer in a small hospital room. The whole experience was difficult, especially for Campbell. He was too young to understand the need for those itchy and sore compression bandages, and all we could do was try and distract him with games and toys and lots of love and cuddles. By the end of his stay we knew every inch of the ward well. We found all the hiding places during our endless games and in our attempts to find a small corner where we could snatch a few minutes of privacy and peace. The staff viewed us as a permanent fixture on their normally short-stay ward. When we left the ward for the final time, we then faced a short wait for the area to heal before the internal components of the implant could be switched on and the external magnetic piece attached.

We returned to Manchester a month later for that much-anticipated day. Before Campbell's implant was switched on we were warned that he might react with shock and cry; that he might be fascinated by the sound, or he might show no outward reaction at all. Sitting with him as the audiologists began to turn the electrodes on using a computer, we scanned his face for a reaction. Typically Campbell, it wasn't dramatic. He showed movement towards noise and some interest, but did not seem overly affected by it. Time would tell how he would respond to the sound and develop his listening skills to utilise it.

Within weeks he was copying sounds and trying to communicate using babble and attempts at words. One of his first was an imitation of 'walk, walk,

walk', whilst playing with a wind-up toy, in a delightful American accent he had borrowed from the therapist doing his rehabilitation sessions at the time. From that day to this Campbell hasn't looked back; his progress has been phenomenal. He very quickly developed age-appropriate use and understanding of language, and to listen to him speak you would hear no difference in his speech compared to that of his peers. He transformed from an exceptionally shy child who avoided engaging with others into a child who wanted adult attention, who wanted to ask them questions and engage with them. With his friends he finds it harder, but he enjoys getting caught in adventure scenarios with those he is closest to and loves nothing more than digging for buried treasure with them in the dirt! We have been so lucky; his cochlear implant has been a true success and well worth the angst we put ourselves through in making the decision.

Following Campbell's operation, another situation within our family came to a head and decisions needed to be made. Lee and I were finding it increasingly difficult to parent the children together as a couple. Our family scenario was so different than the one we had imagined when we started our life together. In adjusting to it and dealing with it in different ways, we lost the common bond that holds couples together. Instead, we moved further apart. Unable to reach out and pull it back together, we separated and eventually divorced. It was not a decision we took lightly or without the boys' needs in mind. We both love the boys, and we maintain cordial links and share information freely for their benefit. To some people's surprise, we can be seen doing things together such as watching the nativity at school and laughing at the boys' triumphs and mishaps. It's not perfect, but we try hard. From that point on, though, my journey was to become lonely for a while as I began caring for the boys as a single parent.

During the assessment process for Campbell's implant, I had another big decision to make about whether I should return to work. Following the boys' diagnosis, I had taken extended maternity leave to allow us time to adjust to our situation and settle the family. Now the time was fast approaching when a decision needed to be made. I had returned to work part-time, three days per week, after having Cameron, and this had worked for us. I had time with Cameron and he also benefitted from time to socialise with other children. The prospect of returning to work following Campbell's arrival, in light of my commitments to appointments and meeting the boys' individual needs, seemed less possible – especially considering Campbell's upcoming operation and subsequent rehabilitation. Should I stay at home and look after them full-time? Was that where my place now needed to be? If I did, could we afford it? There were so many questions which needed to be thought through. This is a difficult decision for many families, though for some there are few options because their financial commitments or career may leave little room for them to manoeuvre.

The time since the boys' diagnosis had taken a lot from me. Because I'm a professional in an associated field of expertise, sometimes others would make assumptions about my knowledge – and their doing so transferred seemingly more pressure onto my shoulders. It made me feel like I should know what I was doing at all times in terms of the boys' progress and development. This feeling, plus my own individual desire for perfection and my belief that I could do everything, left me feeling constantly weighed down. Now, a small part of me felt a desperate desire to return to work – to be in a position where it was not my own children's development I would be focussing on, where I could hand over that responsibility for a short period of time and focus on other people's problems instead. At work I could be in control and sure of myself instead of constantly wondering if I was doing the right thing.

I was very lucky to be part of a supportive department; on initially hearing about the boys' deafness they had appreciated that this situation needed flexibility. When I talked with my managers about returning to work, I was honest with them regarding appointments and my desire to be there with the boys and meet their needs in the best way I could. My experiences as a parent also drove me to want to make a difference in how parents are perceived by professionals and included within the therapy process. Having experienced first-hand the parental side of the fence, I knew there were areas where shared understanding and collaboration could enhance the situation for both parties and, more importantly, for the children involved. I was keen for our department to explore the support we gave to the families we worked with and to see how we could empower them with more knowledge.

At that time, we were about to embark on a new form of parent training. We would be giving information, examples, and activity ideas to the parents, who could use them at home with their children on a more frequent basis in their everyday lives than we could in therapy sessions. To implement the parent training sessions, my manager needed someone on the staff to commit to working evenings so that parents who worked during the day would have the opportunity to attend. Somehow the perfect situation had arisen: I could incorporate the evening sessions as part of my hours. It meant less time away from the boys, as they would be asleep during the evenings I was working, and I would have that small amount of space I needed for me. Those evening sessions were fulfilling to me and made me a better parent to the boys at that time. I was able to share information and experiences with those parents, and it was satisfying to know they were leaving the sessions with some extra insight and confidence in how to approach their child's communication difficulties.

Over time I have changed my hours to accommodate the boys' schooling and needs. Now that I am married to my second husband, Matt, and have a daughter, Emma, I'm not working for the present time; as a family we looked at our situation and that seemed to be the best arrangement. We feel that at this time in our lives I need to be home to provide a stable schedule around which we can plan appointments, homework, social opportunities for the children, and sundry other things. Right now, we would not function so well if we had the added demand of my working.

I believe the key to my decisions about work over the past nine years has been to look at each one, without being too rigid, as the best fit for that time. Our situation has changed so much year-on-year, and it's been crucial to look for the optimal decision at each time as part of a fluid transition. Nothing is set in stone. What is right for one family is not necessarily right for another, and what is right for us now may not be so in the future. Many people will have views on this issue, and some will be more vocal than others. From the outside, where it does not directly impact their daily life and they do not have as much emotion tied up in the outcome, it is easy for them to believe they know what is best. Some feel that families should be able to cope and have both parents out working. Others express the complete opposite view, believing that in this situation there should be no thought of looking to take on a work commitment in addition to the family's needs. These views can muddy the waters for families who are trying to find the best solution for their unique situation.

Only recently I was talking to a mum who has four children, two of whom are deaf. For part of each week she does child minding in their home, and she was questioning whether in light of her children's current needs, and possibly increasing future needs, she was being greedy by continuing with this work. In allowing herself something else to focus on besides her daily concerns, and a way of supplementing the family income, she worried that she was neglecting the needs of her children or that others could perceive it that way. As we talked around the subject, we decided that only she and her husband could accurately ascertain what was right for their family at the time. Anyone else who had supplied an opinion did not have information regarding all the factors involved. We also determined that it would be alright for her and her husband to say to themselves that whilst this situation was suitable for now, it might not always be the case, and they can revisit and revise their decision as needed. Whilst some decisions have finite time constraints and can be made only once, others can be modified.

The more complex choices we face involving our children with difficulties have to be dealt with alongside all the more routine decisions all parents face, such as whether our children should have certain immunisations or be christened, or at what age and how they should be potty trained, to name but a few. All of these take time to think through whilst mulling over family anecdotes about these issues and considering the best choice to make. At times it can feel like we simply move from one decision to the next, constantly weighing pros versus cons and benefits versus risks, always trying to make the wise choice for our children.

Often, the decisions we need to make pertaining to our children's well-being and their future feel like they have been plucked straight from the pages of a Jodi Picoult novel. Just as her characters face seemingly impossible decisions where they must make choices or accept things which are perilously close to the boundaries of their beliefs, or which others may challenge or deem misguided, we find ourselves in similar plights. This may sound dramatic, but I believe it's how many of us feel. There seem to be no right answers, just a series of choices, and we are constantly faced with seeming moral dilemmas.

We must trust in ourselves and our ability to make the best decisions we can with the information we have. We cannot later measure our decisions based on hindsight and actual outcomes – this knowledge was not available to us at the time. It is difficult to remember this, and it is easy to give in to that tiny nagging voice of doubt that asks, did I do the right thing? If we dwell too long on this, however, we are not able to fully commit to the decision we have made and live one moment at a time. Our decision may very well lead to the promising place we believed it would, but we will only find out if we move forward.

Trust

I am not afraid of storms for I am learning to sail my ship.
– Louisa May Alcott

This is a difficult chapter for me to write. I feel like I am standing at the rim of a volcano, looking down at ten years' worth of bubbling red-hot lava. This volcano is a place inside me where I have had to store frustrations along the way. Sometimes an event sparks the lava and I can feel the embers glowing, starting the fire in my belly. I have needed this lava to sustain me, to keep me fighting for my boys. But because I am also very aware of the damage it can do, I am working to dim these embers, and I hope the volcano will go dormant. To this end, in this chapter I will endeavour to circumnavigate the rim of this volcano without plunging to its full depth, for reasons of health, safety, and sanity!

Over time, our culture has left behind the tradition of extended families all living together or near each other, and of older family members delivering new babies within the home, passing down remedies for ailments from generation to generation; making prognoses and diagnoses on any given condition based on the family's past experience and hearsay tales from others. Then, somehow, everyone muddled through. Today, however, many of those in Western society live in smaller discrete family units separated from the rest of their family by miles, countries, and continents.

Because many people are now more isolated from an extended family than they would have been in the past, and because research and knowledge in so many areas of medicine has increased, a higher level of professional involvement has become necessary. The knowledge of medical professionals provides new options and avenues of hope, but it also leads to a medicalization of society in which families naturally turn to doctors and other health professionals, who are perceived to hold so many of the answers to their questions, to help them cope and navigate life.

As more and more aspects of life, even everyday problems and conditions that were previously dealt with within the family and the community, become treated as medical problems and conditions, people become accustomed to consulting a professional to tell them why something has happened and how it must be treated. There are those who feel that this shift to medicalization is a form of social control. The general public are giving away their independence and power to professionals and, ultimately, corporations that will then allow decisions to be swayed by economic considerations rather than the optimal well-being of the people affected by those decisions.

These days, families with children with difficulties have to welcome a parade of professionals into their lives and homes. They help us navigate unexpected challenges and offer assessment and guidance so our children are supported in their development, and we usually appreciate their efforts and sometimes come to feel like we don't know how we'd get on without them.

But whom do we turn to when a situation is not as it should be – when our children appear to be struggling, when they seem to be receiving inadequate or inappropriate support for their needs, when all is not as we were advised it should be? What do we do when we intuitively know our child is not being viewed as a whole person or that his needs are not being met?

As parents, we are driven to explore the different opinions and choices open to us and our children. To turn from that option would be to become blinkered – the way of the world has changed, and we all have to change with it. We also want to trust that the people we turn to for information and explanations of the choices available – the so-called professionals – are accurate, observant, and well versed in their field.

After the experiences many parents have had on their journey, however, trust is something they feel unable to give readily to those working with their children. Each family's experiences are unique, and from the outside it may be impossible to detect when that automatic trust of professionals and their skills and intentions was shattered. But once trust is shattered, every interaction with a professional from then on can be a difficult experience for the family. They need the expertise, advice, and opinions about their child and his or her difficulties that professionals can give, but they are not able to fully trust what they are told.

This can be difficult for the professionals, too; they firmly believe they have the child's best interests at heart, plus they are backed by their educational or medical knowledge and qualifications. It can be challenging to have the family questioning them and their expertise. Depending on their experience with families who have children with difficulties, professionals can vary greatly in their level of understanding of this challenging path, so the eventual outcome of their interventions can also differ.

I have a friend named Gill whom I have known for five years now, and trust is a common theme in many of our discussions. People expect her to trust their judgement to do with her son, but because of her experience in the past she finds herself unable to do so and is constantly on alert, questioning what she's told. Her distrust is understandable: her son, Kallum, was born prematurely and spent a substantial amount of time in and out of hospital as a baby. Seeing differences in Kallum's development compared to her older daughter's steady progress, Gill grew more and more concerned at Kallum's delay in developing communication skills and interacting with the world around him. Through assessment she was told he had good hearing but was showing signs of Autistic Spectrum Disorder, and he subsequently started at a school with appropriate provision for this. Just two months shy of his fifth birthday, however, Kallum had his hearing retested by a different doctor and was found to have a moderate to severe hearing loss, worse in his left ear than his right, which required him to use two hearing aids to access the sound levels of normal speech.

For Gill, this brought relief that Kallum's needs could now be addressed accurately and hope that he would begin to progress. But it also brought anger, frustration, and sadness about the time Kallum had spent in a quieter world, withdrawn from those around him. For years they had been treating the wrong problem, walking along the wrong path, led by the professionals they had trusted. Now steps would have to be retraced to follow a completely different fork in the road. This new path would take time for their family to adjust to; Kallum would need to become accustomed to sound and the strange sensation of ear moulds, and Gill would need to master caring for the equipment. The emphasis would have to be shifted to focus on different targets, and changes would have to be made to their environment to promote ease of hearing. Whilst Gill and the rest of the family were prepared to take on the challenge this new path offered, they also carried the burdens of time lost and of no longer trusting those who were supposed to advise and guide them.

Kallum's placement was changed to a hearing resource base, which he attends with my eldest son and which is attached to a mainstream school. Over the past five years his speech has developed beyond belief. The day he realised that my name wasn't actually 'hamster' and shouted across the playground 'Tamsin' instead, Gill and I looked at each other and wanted to cheer and cry in the same moment. I would never again be 'hamster' – and I was rather partial to that nickname! Kallum's hearing and listening skills had developed to a level that he could self-correct and hear more accurately. Yet despite Kallum's progress, it is clear why even to this day, Gill and her husband find it so difficult to trust what professionals tell them.

I am aware that every family's story, situation, and child are unique. There are many parents of children with difficulties who are walking similar paths to mine, but for whom the path is more straightforward, with smooth transitions between different sections and adequate and consistent support. I hope their positive experiences continue, and I do not want to send the message to those families that they will inevitably face obstacles on their journey similar to those mentioned in this chapter.

The emphasis here is not to highlight scare stories. It is a chance for us as parents to show a brief glimpse of our vulnerability. For many of us, it is something we do not reveal when attending reviews and appointments or receiving theories, test results, and diagnoses. To help explain our behaviour, I believe there should be an amendment to the phrase 'fight or flight' so often used to describe people's reactions when cornered or unsure. In some circumstances, it needs to be expanded to 'fight, flight, or break down completely here and now and not know how to begin to put the pieces back together'. It's slightly more long-winded, I know, but very accurate for many of us! In situations where we may appear to be aggressive, strident, suspicious, negative, or dismissive, and very much within the 'fight' bracket, it is often because the only other option we have is 'break down' – and whilst it is healthy to release our emotions, it can be scary to do so when we don't know how we can pull it all together again. So we use the default 'fight' mechanism for self-preservation in situations that we can't handle or find unfair or futile. This is where the lava I mentioned at the beginning of this chapter drives us forward and allows us to continue doing what needs to be done while protecting us from showing our vulnerability to the outside world.

My friend Janine talks openly about how she unintentionally sabotages meetings with professionals when she finds herself falling into that 'fight' mind-set. Janine's son attends a mainstream school and has a diagnosis of Asperger's syndrome. The diagnosis is relatively recent, though the family had been concerned about Adam's situation for many years. The family are now focussed on helping Adam cope with his awareness of his difficulties and the dynamics of his interactions with others that are becoming more obvious, and important, to him as he grows older. Adam is my favourite conversation partner for discussing the latest Liverpool FC gossip and scores with. He devours football stats and keeps me sharp! He struggles, however, to have the same style of conversation with his peers. He is adept at having these discussions with adults and following their cues to move on to a different topic, but he struggles to translate these skills to chatting with children of his own age. As he grows into his teenage years, an already awkward time, this difficulty in his use of social cues with peers, and its results, confuses him. What wasn't obvious to him as a younger child is now conspicuous.

Often Janine and her husband are faced with new ways in which Adam's difficulties impact him at school and in his relationships with peers. They strive for him to be understood and supported in a way that is sensitive to his needs,

The boys just after diagnosis

Cameron and Campbell the weekend before Campbell's first operation

Campbell after his implant, wearing his equipment. You can see the coil held on his head by the magnet

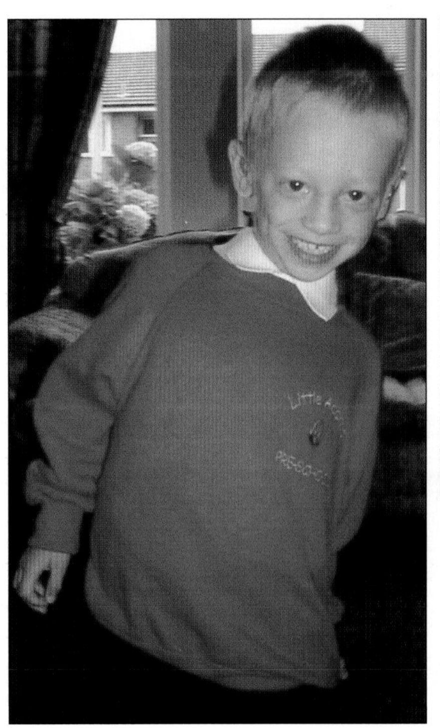

Cameron starting pre-school, 2004

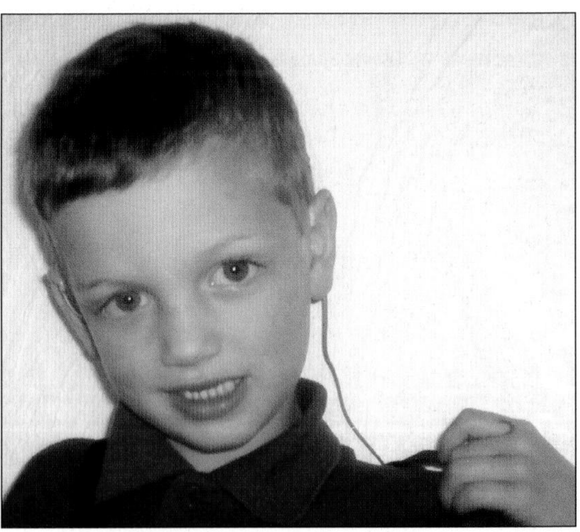

Campbell starting pre-school, 2005

Cameron having fun with his friends Luke and Daniel

We love Halloween in our house; Campbell and I carving pumpkins

The boys having fun on a ride at the Safari Park on a visit to Scotland

Cameron and I having fun on rope swings, the implants haven't stopped the boys doing much

Snowman-making

The boys are growing up now, 2009

Paddling on holiday

Campbell blowing out the candles, you can see his cochlear implant with the wiring to his back pack going under his t-shirt

Cameron with his friend Adam leaving Anfield having watched Jamie Carragher's testimonial match, an exciting evening

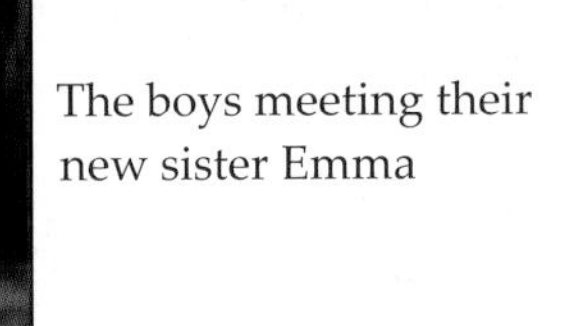

The boys meeting their new sister Emma

Cameron holding Emma

Campbell with Emma just before he swapped his harness for an on the ear processor. Having worn it since he was two he was so used to it being there that when it went he missed it!

The boys; as cheeky now as they've ever been!

Me and my boys

but that builds the self-esteem that is essential for him as a ten-year-old fast approaching secondary school. Unfortunately, in his current school setting, the support in place is at times flawed or doesn't allow for unseen variables, and it fails to prevent incidents which Adam finds hard to deal with. For example, when changing for PE, Adam has a system for organising his clothes when he removes them so he can get dressed when the session is finished. As this is an area in which he does not require support, there is no adult supervision provided at this time. During some typical boy pranks and fun, however, some of the children in the class hid items of clothing from Adam's pile. His routine was thrown off – not only were his things not where he expected them to be, but once retrieved they were out of order. This left his internal system for the order of his day off-kilter, with emotional repercussions.

In discussing these incidents with the school, trying to anticipate other potential stumbling blocks and ensuring there is still a focus on developing Adam's skills to deal with them, Janine struggles to balance her feelings. She feels frustrated at the limits to what is proposed and then what is actually done and is upset by the distress and negativity her son experiences when it all goes wrong. These intense emotions are rooted in her desire to give her child the best opportunity for a happy, positive life, and Janine finds the actual process of meeting with people around a table very difficult to handle. In trying not to expose her feelings and protect herself from showing vulnerability, she instead comes out fighting. Janine's fight response comes out as a defensiveness of her point of view and an abrasive manner towards the professionals there, but this default response of hers can then sabotage the feeling of cooperation with the professionals, who in turn become defensive of their actions and less open to amend or adapt the form of support they provide.

Having worked with children and their families as a Speech and Language Therapist for more than a decade, I am able to see over both sides of the fence, and yet because of the experiences I have had with my children, I still find it difficult to rationalise others' motives and trust their opinions when I am in the parent role. Objectively, I know this mistrust is wrong, and that every professional I have worked with has always thought they have the child's best interests in mind and endeavoured to fulfil their part of the process to meet the child's needs. Professionals are trained in their specialist area and use that knowledge to assess and observe in order to formulate an opinion. They must then communicate this opinion to parents, other professionals, and additional relevant people in reports, meetings, and decision-making processes. Sometimes, however, this opinion can become lost in translation between professional and parent, causing problems and mistrust.

When professionals do convey their professional opinions, they must consider the child holistically and as part of a family. This does not necessarily change the content of what needs to be recommended as appropriate for the child, but the way it is presented should be sensitive to and acknowledge the needs of the family also. Parents can be desperate for a decisive answer to help them move forward; they know something is wrong with their child and need clarification and justification of their fears. But there are also some parents who aren't emotionally ready for blunt news, perhaps because they entered the assessment process without knowing why it was necessary. In both cases it is not always possible to protect them or give them the answer they need, and that is the unfortunate truth that professionals have to live with. However, parents see information and advice regarding their child in relation to their particular family circumstance, the varying needs of their other children, and as well as work commitments and commitments to other family members. All of this could be more readily accounted for and appreciated by professionals.

As a professional myself I have had contact with numerous families. I remember many of them fondly, but one mum in particular stays in my mind. Part of my role involved working with children with multiple and varied areas of need, including speech, language and social difficulties. In our assessments, several professionals would come together to give recommendations over appropriate school placement and the additional support the child requires. Feedback was generally discussed in a group meeting with the parent where a proposal would be made for the child's future school placement. In this particular family, there was more than one child who had special needs that the family were trying to meet. Having established what was good for one child the week before, the mum then attended the meeting regarding one of her other children. Once all opinions were given, the proposed placement named, and the reasons for it discussed, the mum turned in tears to all the professionals sitting around the table and said, 'You don't know what this is like, how hard it is, keeping the children apart, not having them together; you don't have to make decisions like this'.

In that moment I knew every emotion she was feeling, the pressure to do what was best for each of her children, to meet each child's specific needs while also meeting the needs of the family unit. I could feel the burden she had on her shoulders and the pain she felt at the situation evolving around her and over which she had little control. Her way of dealing with it, a fight response, put blame on those giving the advice that was turning her life upside down. Of course, I did know what it was like, I did know how hard it was, yet at that moment I don't think her knowing that could have helped her. She was processing something so difficult, juggling it all in her head and feeling the grief of the situation all at once, and in that moment nothing could take it away. She needed to vent her frustration in order to keep some semblance of control. Professionals need to look past the fight response that so many parents use and see the vulnerable individuals within. People who are managing to just about hold things together by taking a vocal approach, need tolerance from professionals so they can move forward in acceptance.

At times, despite our best efforts, the dam breaks. Many of my friends and I prefer to save our tears for when we are alone or for when we are with those we are close to, but sometimes we can't hold them in. Our fight response gives way, control is lost, and we free-fall down the slide of pent-up emotions. I have cried in frustration, heartache, and sheer exhaustion in meetings with professionals when I would definitely have preferred not to. Sometimes, in the face of the consequences for my children – such as changes in their support level, lack of progress, new areas of concern previously unmentioned – I have been unable to maintain my facade of strength. My tears have sometimes been perceived as an overreaction, or oversensitivity. But more often than not, my upset actually stems from my sense of being alone in my quest for what is best for my boys. Yet again, I interpreted what had been said as an indication that I needed to fight or draw from previous experience to illustrate the boys' difficulties and history. In that moment, the burden of justifying their needs, and not allowing them to be overlooked, rests on me. When I recognize that I hold that responsibility, and as I steel myself to begin, it sometimes becomes overwhelming and my tears start. It feels like as a family and individually we are merely numbers or cases to some people, and there are some days I can't let it simply wash over me. After a time I will pick myself up and continue, but in that moment, I need to turn the tap and release that pressure.

Every family who has children with difficulties will amass a team of professionals around them. This is not optional; it is necessary and unavoidable. The size of this team will vary depending on the child's needs and will include many distinctive and diverse personalities. Over time, different families will feel contrasting emotions about this group around them. Some families will feel that these professionals provide them with shelter and protection, a windbreak from the world of confusion around their child. These professionals earn parents' trust. They are dependable and the family can sense their commitment to their child as an individual rather than a case that needs to be managed. Other families may struggle more with the presence of these professionals. They might perceive the team around them as blocking their way to what they feel they need, forming a barricade to services they deem imperative for their child, a wall they find hard to surmount, or simply a puzzling maze they find confusing, impossible to navigate through and full of dead ends.

Most parents find that there are certain members of their child's professional team with whom they can more easily build trust and whom they can rely upon. Often, these are the people who are part of the team over a longer term and who have more experience. Even if in the past there have been negative interactions with professionals, there are those who will over time prove themselves to be invaluable allies for the child. Learning this has been a gradual process for me as a parent, but I have found that there are certain people I instinctively reach out to when a situation transpires. I know that they have a good knowledge of my children and their strengths, needs, and personality quirks. I know they will help me work around any area of difficulty from different viewpoints to reach a satisfactory conclusion.

As a family, we are lucky to still have the same paediatrician who was assigned to the boys at diagnosis. He has known the boys for nearly a decade and seen them grow from babies into pre-teens. He has been a fantastic point of focus to which we've drawn all the information gathered over the years, a familiar face that I trust completely with the boys' well-being. When the boys were small we had a lot of input from our local Teacher of the Deaf service and Speech and Language Therapy service. These people supported me and grew to know the boys almost as well as I did. They did all they could to help them achieve their potential, sometimes against stacked odds.

There was one lady who visited Campbell weekly in the years before his implant. Each week she would bring a bag of activities to engage him and work on language with him through sign. It became a standing joke that no matter what she did, Campbell would just sit and watch her intently and never participate. But the minute the session finished and she left our house, he would be eager to try all he had just seen – with me, not her. This lady was amazing despite receiving so little feedback during her visits. She came every week, good natured and enthusiastic as ever, and through her visits Campbell learned so much. As he grew she still supported him, always knowing when he was struggling and when he needed a push. I won't name this lady here, but the renowned 'Mrs Purple' knows who she is!

Without those professionals to be confident in and rely upon, my job as a parent would have been infinitely more difficult. Their knowledge of possibilities and internal workings, within their respective systems, gave them an insight which I didn't have. They also have enough detachment to highlight aspects of my children and their development which are invisible to me. The new phrases that they use or their understanding of new concepts don't always jump out at me in between cooking dinner and the many other requests and responsibilities of my day, but professionals can look at a child with fresh eyes and spotlight small areas of progress, or underline areas of concern, that parents are often too close to see.

Only very recently I had a conversation with an audiologist whom I have known for several years. As part of her job she is now seeing families at diagnosis appointments for children who had been identified through the Newborn Hearing Screening as having hearing problems. Our conversation turned into a discussion of the advantages and disadvantages of diagnosing so early, often when the baby is less than three months old. She knows from a theoretical point of view that all evidence points towards early intervention being more successful, but even though she is not a parent herself, she can also see the effects on parents of having to deal with the monumental news of a diagnosis of their child at such a young age. She is observing, on a regular basis, the vast disruption it brings to the normal rhythm and bonding between parents and their new baby. Despite what she knows is correct in the practical sense, her natural instincts are challenging that and heightening her awareness on an individual basis with each family she sees. To her, each child is someone's son or daughter, and this helps her bring careful thought and consideration to each interaction and makes her more successful in communicating and building trust, conveying that she is genuinely there to help both parent and child.

I am sad to say, there may also be encounters with less-considerate professionals on our journey. Perhaps it will be a person who doesn't have an appropriate level of deaf awareness, for example, who whilst examining a child will ask them to remove their hearing aids or implant and then expect a response or ask a question far exceeding the child's language level. Maybe it will be a person who leaves a parent overwhelmed because they do not consider every facet of a child's difficulties and the family's demands when developing expectations of both parent and child. We can also encounter people who are just having a bad day, or who are in a period in their life when they are able to fulfil the requirements of their post but can't summon up the extra interest needed to look at a child and family in a holistic light. As a parent I have found it becomes natural – and crucial – to never lose my focus or become distracted, because I will be the person who can hold the different pieces of the puzzle together when we encounter this type of professional.

So how do we handle these difficult interactions? I'm often reminded of a story about a Cherokee grandmother who is said to have explained to her family that in times of difficulty, you find inside yourself two wolves. These wolves are in battle within your core. One is driven by anger at the situation and seeks to rage and avenge. The other wolf, however, is prompted by an understanding of how a situation could have transpired and professes a kinder viewpoint. Only one can be dominant within you and direct your reactions. When asked by her family which one will win, the Grandmother replied, "The one you feed!" As parents, we have difficulty accepting that we should have to face inept, ineffectual, or blinkered people whilst receiving necessary input for our children. It won't happen every time, and though we should prepare for it, we should not try to pre-empt it. For if we enter interactions from this perspective we then make unfair assumptions that may then lead to the result we feared – a self-fulfilling prophecy.

One of the primary reasons I believe these difficult interactions occur is because of a professional's lack of education or experience in the specific areas in which our children have difficulties. It's not a deliberate act, but rather an unintentional outcome. This is how I can find my focus to draw a deep breath and cope when I find myself in a situation with a professional, where the outcome is insufficient or I have been left discontent. These professionals will not magically acquire the insight I want them to have about my child, as part of a larger family or about the history of his path to date. But if I persevere in enlightening them to my reality in a calm and measured way, this can sometimes assist me in reaching a good outcome. This means acknowledging the wolf inside me that represents my indignation, hurt, and resentment, but trying to move past it to instead feed the other wolf, the one which by being more understanding could lead me to a better outcome for not only my child and my family, but also for other families with whom the professional will interact in the future.

Time, experience, and emotional maturity have got me to a place where I can practice this, most of the time! One Sunday morning I took my elder son to the 'out of hours' doctor to be assessed. He had suffered great pain in his ear through the night and his symptoms could not wait to be seen by our regular doctor the next day. On getting to the clinic we were seen quickly and all was going well. The doctor checked Cameron, found him to have a severe ear infection, and started to write out a prescription for the medicine he felt would manage the infection. In this instance and at this point, Cameron had already received his cochlear implant which meant an open pathway from his inner ear to his brain. I knew that because of his implant, an ear infection could lead to serious complications. Having been through this scenario before, I asked the doctor to contact our local implant centre for advice on our next step. The doctor looked up, disgruntled and offended – he had diagnosed the problem and knew which medicine to prescribe to resolve it. His pleasant disposition was gone; he was clearly not pleased that I was challenging his expertise. He restated his treatment plan, daring me to find the mettle to ask for an additional opinion once again.

By asking him to call the implant centre, I was not disbelieving him; I was following standard medical protocol. It was certainly not the easy option for me, as it could mean a long drive to the hospital, leaving my other children at home, and necessitating the cancellation of all foreseeable plans. In a haze of exhaustion from being up all night with an ill child and frustration born from years of such struggles, I fought against my internal urge to snap at him in anger. Instead, I willed myself to stay calm and in control, to feed and nurture the right wolf. I had to try and remember that all our actions have an impact, and in this moment I could choose what impact to make that might affect future patients' interactions with this doctor. So I repeated my request politely but firmly and reiterated all the reasons.

The doctor picked up the phone with an exasperated sigh, clearly unhappy with this turn in events. I sat calmly and reassured my son. As we waited while he discussed our case with the on-call registrar at the hospital, I calmed. I could then reason that this area was obviously not part of the knowledge the doctor had acquired so far, and his confidence could not handle being questioned. His response to the perceived challenge was inappropriate and hostile, hiding his fear, but that didn't mean I had to respond in the same manner.

As the doctor hung up the phone and turned back to face us, I saw that his demeanour had changed. He told us that the specialist at the hospital needed us to go over and probably stay a couple of nights for treatment. As we left the room the doctor commented quietly, 'It was good that you mentioned referring on; I knew nothing about it'. As Cameron and I crossed the car park together, he turned to me and after a pause said, 'It's good – now that doctor knows more about implants and deafness'. I couldn't have been more proud. Despite his pain and the prospect of further tests, my son had identified the positive that could be taken from what had happened. It is something he will have to deal with for a longer time than I. Focussing on helping him approach challenges in this way also helps me. It keeps me from giving in to the lava of built-up frustration stored in that volcano, so I can walk on more calmly.

Identity

What you think of me, I will think of me. What I think of me, I will be.
– National Deaf Children's Society

'He's not listening to me!' It's a typical refrain heard between siblings in many a house, not just ours. In our house, however, the complaint becomes louder at shower time and bedtime when one of my boys is desperately trying to convey a message to the other to hurry him up, to gain his attention, or for many other reasons. Each boy's indignation at being ignored by his brother is genuine, but each of them is seemingly completely oblivious to the innocent reason behind the lack of response. The reason should be so obvious to them that it still astonishes me when these incidences occur. Both my boys remove their cochlear implants and hearing aids (they usually wear an implant on the left side and a hearing aid on the right) when showering/bathing, swimming, and at bedtime. So at these times and throughout the night they rely instead on lip-reading and signing to communicate. To my bafflement, despite each boy's own lifelong experience, neither of them seems to understand why his brother cannot hear him at these times.

When my boys were diagnosed as deaf it was not a complete shock; as I have explained earlier, there had been warning signs that all was not as it should be for their hearing, listening, and communication. Because I had seen these signs and had been actively pushing for the boys' assessment and diagnosis, it was a real relief when we finally found out. That relief was mixed in with all the other emotions, but at least we knew what was happening and had a starting point from which to move forward. Then came the bucket of cold water; this was not something we knew much about. I had acquired some knowledge through my training, which logically gave me more of an advantage than some families have, but because it was not the area in which I practiced it had all been distant theory. Now it was time to learn. Like 90 percent of deaf children, our boys had been born to hearing parents. We did not know what they were experiencing or how this affected them first-hand. No one else in our family is deaf, so we had no family experience to draw upon or associate with. We had to find our own way to raise the boys, with this set of difficulties, and to help them be comfortable with themselves and their identity and to find their place in the world. To this day, it is a work in progress, and perhaps it always will be.

Like any parent, my driving force for the boys is my desire for them to develop a positive self-esteem and identity. To encourage this I have had to try and understand the delicate balance between the deaf side of their life and the hearing life they are naturally part of, and then also consider their own personalities, which puts a completely different spin on things!

The Deaf Community feels strongly that for deaf individuals to develop a clear sense of identity, pride in their deafness, and feeling of belonging to a community, they should be brought up in Deaf culture, perhaps even without the use of technology to improve their hearing. In the past, deaf children were often sent away, even at a young age, to a boarding school where they would be cared for and educated with their peers. It's hard to imagine how difficult it was for those families whose only option for their children was to send them away from the family unit, often to a school out of the local area. The practices at some of these schools just added to the sorrow I feel for those children and their families. For example, in some places the children were known by numbers, not by their names. They each had to respond to their number and use it to identify themselves. In circumstances where deaf people were not individuals but numbers to be accounted for, and where they lacked the influence and support of their families, the origins of a community took hold. Naturally, that community continued into adulthood as a cultural group that held a shared identity, whilst recognising the stark differences that isolated them from the world around them.

Times have changed and so has the world of the Deaf Community; there is now more potential for today's deaf children. The emphasis in education is now on supporting deaf children, as much as is possible, within their local mainstream school. This makes them more isolated from their deaf peers but encourages their integration with hearing peers in their immediate environment. There is the option, in some regions, of utilizing a hearing resource base that is attached to a mainstream school; in this way the children have access to a group of deaf peers and specialist teachers and sign support whilst also being integrated into classes with hearing peers. For some children this is an ideal mix, but it may still require them to travel daily to a school outside their local area. In addition, there are still a small number of day and boarding schools where deaf children are educated together.

One family my children and I had been close to over the initial years, following diagnosis, actually moved to an area where they could best meet their daughter's educational needs whilst still keeping her within the family unit. Esme had numerous medical complications after having been born prematurely as a twin. She had undergone several surgeries and was still very medically dependant when it was realised that she was also profoundly deaf. Esme had bilateral cochlear implants when she was three years old, and she attended the area's mainstream resource base. Despite the benefit of using the implants and Esme's parents following every avenue to build on her skills, her educational and language development progressed slowly, and the gap between Esme and both her deaf and hearing peers was growing. Her parents started to look to how Esme's needs could be met at secondary level. Her family had the option of sending Esme away to attend a deaf school which could support her, but she would have to attend as a weekly boarder and only see her family at the weekend – or they'd have to choose an alternative with much wider implications.

It was an unenviable quandary, fraught with emotion. Their eventual move from the north-west of England to the south coast, a distance of hundreds of miles, has enabled their daughter to attend a deaf school as a day pupil whilst living at home with her family. Her mum and dad made this decision, which also required the relocation of their other two (hearing) children to new schools, because they could not consider sending their daughter away. As parents we now expect to have the option to not have to send away our children, to not exclude them from family life. They can exist in the very heart of it instead.

This cultural shift has allowed more deaf children to stay within the family, but it has also affected their interactions with other deaf children and adults. Luckily, technological advances such as text messages, Skype, and webcams allow youngsters who grow up with infrequent contact with deaf peers to stay connected; a series of texts can catch them up on the latest news at times when it is not possible to meet face-to-face.

Some regions have more active Deaf Communities than others. Some members of the Deaf Community believe that hearing parents should respect their views because deaf children may have those same views when they are older, and because as Deaf adults they have more first-hand knowledge and information about deafness. I certainly agree; they know and share things with my sons that I could never know and will not experience. All I can do is help them grow into their own identity by learning about these views and trying to marry them with the hearing world the boys exist in.

I feel that my boys need to be comfortable with their deafness and acknowledge it as a central element in their lives. I know that not all families with deaf children feel this way, though; some families try to integrate their children as fully as possible into the hearing world, with as little emphasis on the hearing loss as possible. This can take the form of not wanting them to socialise with deaf peers, having them wear long hair and clear moulds to disguise hearing aids, and various other subtle signs. Often families take an aural approach with their child that involves purely listening and speaking with no signing. They may believe that signing will make other people think their child is strange for using his hands to communicate and that using sign will limit the number of people the child can interact with.

For me the decision was easy. Because of my work background, I wanted the boys to have access to communication in as many forms as we could initially provide for them, to reduce their frustration and to help them connect with those around them. We utilised signing, visual timetables, and photo books in addition to developing their listening skills and having them wear hearing aids. Total communication seemed the most logical approach to take. I know, from theory and professional experience, that the use of sign does not limit or stop the development of language in children who have a variety of communication difficulties. Signing is used to support rather than replace an oral communication method. Deaf children tend to develop 'contact sign', where they creatively mix their knowledge of linguistic resources, such as British Sign Language and spoken English, to communicate. Having knowledge of sign as well as being able to communicate orally gives children the capacity to access two cultures and provides a bridge into both communities. Awareness of different forms of communication can also benefit children by giving them an increased sensitivity to the communication needs of others.

There were many challenges as we figured out the best modes of communication for our family. Being in the car with the boys was a particularly difficult part of our day when they were small. They could not hear my voice when I tried to reassure them and could not read my lips while I was facing forward. It was frustrating and unsettling for all of us. Occasionally I used one-handed signs to communicate with them in the back seat and let them know I was still there. One sign I used regularly was our sign for 'two minutes', which the boys understood to mean we were nearly at the end of our journey. The sign itself was simple: I put my hand in their line of sight in the middle of the car and showed them two upright fingers with the others bent over. It was only after a fellow driver slowed down as he passed, shaking his head and making gestures at me, that I realised what I had been doing. For months I had appeared to be showing an offensive gesture to every car which had driven behind me. Oh, the shame and lesson learned!

Our families were not fluent in sign, but everyone played their part in helping to varying degrees and with varying results. In reminiscing recently with my stepmother, Sharron, we were talking about how she used to get on the floor to play with the boys when they were little, occasionally asking for specific signs to use with them and the rest of the time just using her hands as visually as she could to convey meaning. They muddled through splendidly, sometimes leading to misunderstandings with hilarious consequences, but they enjoyed the play and the connection with a familiar adult. Now Sharron uses that experience in her work as a librarian; if a deaf adult comes into her library, more often than not she is called on to communicate to them. She says her experience with the boys means she can have full conversations and successfully meet the requests of these adults using sign, her own quasi sign, and other communication skills. It is a part of her job that she finds fulfilling. It is such a nice feeling to know that in their own indirect way the boys are influencing deaf awareness for others.

Deaf awareness means promoting deafness in a hearing world. It helps people communicate more effectively with a deaf person by making them aware of the difficulties a deaf person faces. Often, when people talk to a deaf person, a very stereotypical image comes to mind and they believe that they can best convey their message by shouting and talking in drawn-out syllables (think of all those comedy sketches where someone is trying to talk to an elderly relative with hearing problems). In fact, this approach often impedes the deaf person's ability to understand what is being said more than it helps them. Deaf people need others to slow down when speaking to them, but not too much, and to indicate the topic they want to speak about. Using a clear and slightly louder, but not shouting, voice in a quiet environment is ideal. It is helpful for speakers to direct their speech to the deaf person's aided or implanted side and to position their face so it is not in shadow (to allow for lip-reading).

Every day, four babies are born deaf, with varying degrees of hearing loss, but because of geographical distribution they can be very isolated from each other. Cameron and Campbell have each other, but I wanted them to grow up with both hearing and deaf peers. They will always need people with shared experiences whom they can turn to in life. Just as they need to share with their hearing peers in the characteristic adventures and encounters, of each stage of life, they will also need that unique affinity I envisage they will find with their deaf peers. We have been lucky in our decision to have both boys attend a hearing resource base in a mainstream school, Cameron for all of his primary schooling and Campbell until the age of 8 when he transferred to our local primary school. Although it is out of our immediate area and they required daily transport to get there, it has met the boys' need to not be the only deaf students. They both had at least two deaf peers in their class along with twenty or so hearing children and they both had access to classes with both spoken and sign language. In Cameron's nursery nativity the students signed every song they sang, and I sat in equal parts amazed and mortified as the whole class participated, with one exception: my son, who was too overcome by the whole situation to sign a single word! It reinforced how well my child could be included and encouraged to participate, even in this mainstream setting. It was a powerful message to soothe a worried mother's mind.

In addition to having them interact with deaf peers at school, I have been keen for the boys to socialise with deaf peers of all ages in free time also. I want them to have the option to participate in the Deaf Community as they grow and to know they can turn to this community when and if they feel the need. When they are more mature and know themselves a bit better they may decide not to engage with the Deaf Community, but for now I see it as my job to keep that avenue open.

I've seen many ways in which the boys have benefitted from contact with deaf peers. When Cameron first had his cochlear implant, it caused him intense nerve pain for the first thirty seconds after he put it on. We worked with school in encouraging his use of it, but we were all struggling. Then Cameron, age four and a half, found his first deaf role model. One of the eldest deaf children in the school also had an implant. He was in his final year of school and was a prefect, so he was frequently visible in assemblies and on the playground. He started to give Cameron a wink or a thumbs-up when he saw him wearing his implant. The school's Teacher of the Deaf rang me after the first couple of times it happened to share what she had seen. Cameron was so proud of the attention and praise from this older boy with whom he could identify, that he apparently just beamed at each occasion. He started to wear his implant more and more consistently. What had been achieved by a wink and a thumbs-up was far greater than the words and promises we adults had tried. The value of shared identity had won through. Now, after all this time, I recognise that my boys are, as older deaf children, role models for the younger ones.

Both boys have over time found their own identities with their deafness and their hearing and signing worlds, but as is typical with siblings, it is very different for each of them. Cameron, who has always been more reliant on sign, switches easily between speech with his hearing peers and sign with profoundly deaf peers at the resource base and at events with other deaf children. At home he uses mainly speech but will throw sign in to add emphasis or when questioning, and often relies on it when having new things explained. He has a strong identity as a deaf individual but also takes his place in the hearing world where he attended all the local playgroups as a baby and toddler, has played football with mainstream peers for years, and attended Beavers at the local church.

Cameron has had moments of questioning his life and its complications, though, saying things like "I don't want to be deaf anymore" or "I don't want to have to change my batteries and miss out!" It tore my heart in two to hear those words and know that he was hurting. I had to learn quickly and find a way to respond that would encourage him to perceive himself in a positive way and not be worried about how he compares with others. He needed to know that although we couldn't change the fact that he was deaf, it wasn't a failing that had to be fixed in order for him to have a full and satisfying life. It is part of him, and because he is deaf, he as an individual holds so many unique skills and qualities. No, that wasn't the answer a seven-year-old wanted to hear, but we talked it through and added humour to lighten the situation for him, pointing out benefits like being able to switch off and shut his eyes to avoid being told off by his parents!

Campbell is still more of a conundrum. He is more confused about his identity and where he fits in the world at large. Because he has been using his cochlear implant successfully for the majority of his life, he frequently identifies himself as hearing rather than deaf. From the age of two he has been able to use his hearing sense to aid his progress in the world. It took him from being a little boy who was isolated in his world of silence, dependant on me alone and cautious of the world around him, to a child who wants to learn and soak in everything he can. He was entranced by the sources of newly heard noises and literally ran forwards to be a part of them. He has knowledge of sign language from the early days, but he long ago moved on from using it, preferring to use the vast verbal vocabulary that he amasses daily from copious reading and discussions. Campbell will still follow instructions and ask questions for me to respond to in sign at night, but typically will not respond in sign himself.

A few years ago, I took the boys to a New Year's Eve party at a friend's house. I had arranged that I could settle the boys to sleep in my friend's spare bedroom when they were ready to rest. Cameron lay down and, as he usually does, drifted off to sleep without issue. I lay down beside Campbell, who finds sleep harder, his mind often too busy to switch off. As I lay beside him he began to move his hands. I watched Campbell sign the whole of the Christmas carol 'Away in a Manger', and it was one of the most beautiful things I had ever seen. He was so fluent and sure, doing it for himself, not an audience. When he finished, he turned on his side and fell asleep. I choose to interpret this to mean that he secretly needs to know that he still has that skill, a safety net, in case he needs it. Yet it's a skill he prefers to keep private and not let people know about, lest they use it to stereotype him.

One of the most important traits I hope the boys will develop, is a resilience and strength of character to believe in themselves and the identity they grow into. They will need it. As I have mentioned, times have changed, as have others' perceptions of deafness and other disabilities. However, as is generally the way with change, it is gradual. Tides of more informed opinion often ripple out as people gain experience, yet these waves don't reach everyone and islands of ignorant views still remain where there is a greater value placed on being or appearing 'normal'. I know that, despite a more inclusive society and workplaces full of anti-discrimination policies, my sons are going to need to prove themselves over and over to show they are adequate and as good as, if not better than, the next person to remain in contention in the workplace, in friendships, and in relationships.

Only recently this was reinforced to me at a school event. Parents, professionals, dignitaries, and assorted others had been invited to celebrate the opening of the new building for the hearing resource base. This building had purpose-built classrooms and extra rooms which were set to the side to provide a quiet environment for listening and communication exercises. Amidst an atmosphere of goodwill and pride in the school's achievement, I sat at one of the tables to listen to the presentations and the children's contributions. Beside me sat another parent, a sign language interpreter, and two deaf adults who regularly helped the children and their families develop their signing skills.

Following the head teacher's speech, an older man approached the front to take his turn. This gentleman had been the head teacher when the resource base had initially opened many years before. In his speech he talked about the wonders of technology currently available to assist Deaf children, such as hearing aids and cochlear implants. This then led to his commenting, unfortunately, on what would have become of the children in front of him without the benefit of this technology. How much better it was now that hearing aids and implants are becoming more discreet and less visible to the world at large. In listening, I became increasingly uncomfortable that all this was being said and interpreted to the deaf adults beside me who had made the choice to live their life without technology – and were doing so to the benefit of our children. Experiencing this man's comments in the company of deaf adults, I could see clearly how the Deaf Community's views were formed. I understood their need to take pride in their deafness and dispel the myth of deafness being something that needs to be fixed, and why they campaign so aggressively for a wider understanding of their views.

This speech was also delivered in front of our children, who are growing daily in their self-knowledge. I believe it is inappropriate to speak in positive terms only about their equipment and thus detract from their deaf identity. This was his view of how life would be better for the children, and he had valid points about the benefits technology had brought. Yet, despite his years of working with deaf children and their families he had not developed a balanced view of the true value all human beings, deaf and hearing, can bring to the world if supported in being confident in their abilities, be their contributions by speech, sign, text, e-mail, written word, assisted communication, or their actions.

To build their self-esteem and confidence in their own identity, all children need to be valued for who they are. This will enable them to carve their own way as they get older. This support naturally begins within the family, with parents and siblings. Because there are a number of causes of hearing loss, it is not surprising that there is often a mix of both deaf and hearing adults and children within one family. Hearing children may have their own areas of difficulty in life; they could have motor difficulties, struggles with particular subject areas, or need extra focus for an assortment of different reasons, but there is a clear distinction when one child has a far-reaching and obvious difficulty compared to her siblings.

Having both deaf and hearing children in one family is a challenge for parents, who will have to address the identity needs of both their deaf children and their hearing children. It can seem less obvious than the effects on the deaf child's own identity, but having a deaf sibling can affect the hearing children's sense of identity too.

I waited a long time to have a third child. Assuredly this is partially because of the break-up of my first marriage, but I was also waiting for the right time for our family. I had to balance the boys' needs and the time it took to support their development against the time and care a new baby would need. While I was pregnant with Emma, I remember meeting an acquaintance in a waiting room. She commented on my growing bump and then whispered to me that she hoped for my sake that this baby wouldn't be deaf too. How was I to respond? As an overly hormonal pregnant woman, I battled not to cry and shout. I explained briefly that as long as the baby was healthy, we would be grateful. Matt and I entered into the pregnancy with our eyes wide open to the possibility that this baby could be deaf too. Despite him being a different partner, there was still a chance that genetics could cause a hearing difficulty, or some other difficulty. To us, the only issue was hoping for our baby's sake that he or she wouldn't have to go through the operations the boys had. To express a desire for our new baby to not be deaf, felt like a betrayal of the boys – a diminishing of them, their characters, and their achievements.

When Emma was born, all those around seemed focussed on the results of the Newborn Hearing Screening. Our conversations followed predictable patterns with most people: the baby's name, time of birth, weight, is mum OK? And then the inevitable: how did her hearing test go? I know it was a logical concern for those who care about our family, but it was irrelevant to us in our first hours with this brand-new life we had created. She would be perfect to us regardless of the result, just as her brothers are.

Emma passed her hearing test. As a hearing child, she is in the minority in our family. She has hearing parents, of course, but both of her siblings, whom she looks up to and tries to emulate in her own innocent way, are deaf. We are not the only ones with this fusion within their family; I have a close friend who has the same blend of two deaf children and one hearing child at home. So often our focus has to be on our deaf children, their next appointment, or our latest concern. It is only when our days are calmer that we reflect on the effect our family's lifestyle has on our other children.

As the youngest in our family, Emma has attended many, many appointments and reviews pertaining to one or both of her brothers in her first few years of life. She has been there awake, asleep, teething or cheerful. She has been entertained on some days by well-planned activities and snacks for the duration of the meeting. On other days when a more hectic schedule has prevailed, I have resorted to scraps of paper and pens, with the random box of raisins left at the bottom of my bag to suffice as sustenance. She always muddles through. As one of the regular attendees at the meetings commented to me recently, she'd be surprised if Emma did not become a related professional when she grows up because of her experiences so far. In this aspect of life, Emma has been expected to accommodate the needs of her brothers since before she was aware of it happening. She either attends these meetings and appointments with me or I have to leave her behind. Sometimes we can do this so she enjoys special time with her grandparents, but there are days when she is unwell or tired, when either taking her or leaving her with someone else feels unfair, but I have to do it anyway. Cue that maternal guilt again. For other instances, such as in-patient hospital stays with one of the boys, there is no option; I must leave her care to someone else while I care for her brother.

My friend's young hearing son also has two deaf siblings. As he gets older he is noticing more of the 'positive' aspects to his sister and brother's situation, such as extra time away with mum and the attention that is paid to them by the professionals they go to see. At his young age it is hard for him to see the negative side his deaf siblings endure that balances things out. One day on a trip to a DIY warehouse he sat in the trolley facing his mum. As they went down an aisle he heard the noise of a forklift truck in the distance, its sensors beeping as it moved backwards. "What's that noise, Mummy?" he asked. His mum explained the source of the noise. He then responded, "I can't hear it, Mummy, I'm deaf!" This continued for the duration of the store visit and sporadically over the next few days. It was never fully resolved, but was likely shelved in his mind to process at his own pace.

When I was dressing Emma one morning, she turned to me and asked, "Where's my hearing aid?" It is something so routine in our lives, and in her toddler way she wanted to be like her brothers and expected that she should have one too. All of these reactions are typical and vary as each child expresses his or her feelings as a sibling of a deaf child. It is natural for deaf children like my boys to question why they are deaf, and it is equally natural for their hearing siblings to wonder why they aren't. Identities are a two-way street connecting our family. For parents, building these identities separately is a learning process which becomes an art of balancing resentments, cultivating common ground, nurturing an understanding of others' needs, and acknowledging and celebrating the differences which make our family what it is – unique and amazing.

Way of Life

When your mind says give up, hope whispers 'one more try'.
– Anonymous

Happiness, not in another place but this place … not for another hour, but this hour.
– Walt Whitman

Sometimes there comes a moment of clarity, when we regain a perspective we had lost sight of or we are able to see things from a new angle. One such moment came over a glass of wine with my friend Lisa and her sister-in-law Sharon, while sitting on patio chairs in the growing darkness of Lisa's garden. We were hiding in the garden to find some peace for a girlie chat, and our conversation had covered everything from in-laws, to work, to the upcoming royal wedding and how to persuade our husbands that a foreign holiday really was a good idea! Somehow the conversation turned back to a story about how Lisa and I had met our school receptionist in a shop during the holidays, and she had greeted us as friends and passed more than the time of day with us as we queued to pay. Sharon looked at us both and said she hadn't ever seen any of her school office staff, except on one quick trip in to pick up her daughter when she was ill. She wouldn't be able to recognise any of them outside of school, she said. At that moment, an unspoken acknowledgement passed between Lisa and me, a moment of clarity about our unique situations.

It is so easy to forget that ours is a way of life that not everyone knows or could imagine. A life where the head teacher says hello on passing us on the playground and stops to comment on the outcome of Campbell's latest review, the reception staff at school don't ask my name or his when collecting him for weekly appointments, and they notice Emma's latest achievement. They are a central part of our daily life! I recently left a message for the Teacher of the Deaf at Cameron's school to return my call when she could. Upon hanging up I realised I hadn't left my name or number, but then figured the school secretary knew who I was (I suppose it helps having a Scottish accent in the north-west of England!). Sure enough, ten minutes later the teacher called me back.

It is not only a familiarity with the school staff that is a feature of this way of life; there are lots of other unique elements as well. Somehow, as we walk forward on this path, it is easy to forget how different it is from others' paths – and then we wonder at the lack of understanding from people for whom our way of life is so far removed from their own experience.

We all have our own routine in life which we fall into and considerations we make without a second thought. For so many families with children with difficulties, this includes things which others wouldn't think of because they have never needed to. In our family, for example, I carry extra batteries for hearing aids and implants wherever I go. At the first sign of an ordinary ear infection in either of the boys, we plan for a trip to Manchester, over an hour away, where the chances are high that they will have to stay in hospital for IV antibiotics. We have to ensure equipment is removed at the first hint of contact with water in its many forms. (Other parents may not even realize all of the ways water appears in the world of little boys: in water bombs and pistols, torrential rain, canoeing, swimming, assault courses, and amusement rides with water hazards, to name but a few!) Then I need to monitor the children and be in a position to communicate important information to them while the implants are detached (my boys can't hear the lifeguard's whistle while they're in the swimming pool, and with their tendency for mischief it can be needed). The list goes on and on. There is even the comical side, where I see one of my children going into the soft play centre with their implant or hearing aid on and coming out without it, and I know what must be done. More than once I have been the parent who has gone down the big slide into the ball pond and searched its depths for the lost equipment, to the amusement of all the parents watching. I had no other option; it needed to be found. But since the first time it happened, I have always been careful of my clothing choices for these trips – definitely no skirts allowed!

All this is second nature after all these years. I don't tend to register even doing things like negotiating attendance at appointments with whichever child needs to be there and arranging child care and meals for the others whilst I am away, up to four times a week sometimes. Then there's the rescheduling of clashing appointments, attending regular school assemblies and parents' evenings, fitting in GP appointments, plus trips to opticians with broken glasses, days written off with my younger son's migraines, phone calls with a variety of involved professionals, and all the other everyday things that are part of running a family. Some weeks it can be that I am desperate for a break, wishing for the roundabout to stop so I can get off to catch my breath and stop the world from spinning for a moment.

With my daughter, I have had a glimpse of a different type of life. She, bless her, is comparatively low maintenance (although I don't expect this to last – she is female, after all!). Emma has had no hearing difficulties and has reached all developmental milestones without remark or cause for concern. She is a typical walking, talking 'bossy boots'. She may yet encounter areas of life that are difficult for her, but up to this point I have been able to just enjoy her without accounting for and remembering each stage she has gone through, noting each word she has learned or understood, or attending numerous appointments where I feel the need to justify her progress or lack thereof and defend decisions I have made.

Now that I have a hearing child I can see why uninitiated people may wonder at the micro-management required to run this type of life. They observe our need for reassurance, the hesitancy which we can have in trusting our own instincts, and the defensiveness that comes all too quickly to the surface to insist that we are doing the best we can. Those who don't have children with difficulties also see our reliance on outside agencies around seemingly 'normal' areas of life, checking small things that to others would seem of no significance. We might wonder which toy to buy our child for Christmas to aid their development, or whether we should push our child and expect them to be able to cope in a particular situation or instead keep the safety net in place on that occasion. It may seem like over-vigilance or paranoia on our part, but this insecurity comes from not wanting to miss anything we could or should be doing for our children. Often, a situation is new to us, but professionals who have seen this situation so many times before can make a comment or convey a piece of advice which clears up our uncertainty so simply.

It can be a challenge to remember that it is OK to take time to simply enjoy our children, especially when the day-to-day focus of life is on our children's needs and what they struggle with. But as parents it is one of the most important things we can do. Those moments of sunshine, the times when we stop and marvel at the wonders that are our children, will be what get us through. No matter when they come, we must commit fully to those moments and forget targets, goals and development for a while. I cherish simple times with my children, like having all three of them helping to bake in our small kitchen: flour and eggs going everywhere, and mostly in Emma's mouth. Take That's music coming out of the iPod speakers, with all of them dancing around and laughing at their efforts; joining in with the lyrics and then realising the window is open for all the neighbours to hear us! It does all disintegrate into a messy shambles quite rapidly, with children squabbling and a distinct smell of burning cakes, but those precious moments will see me through so much.

Parents of children with difficulties do not lead private lives; we must quickly adapt and lose any inhibitions we may have about others knowing our business. There are so many questions that probe every area of life, some seemingly unrelated to the situation right now. It can seem so trivial to be asked if or how often our children do this or that, and so often we seem to have to answer the same questions over and over to different people. The answers, however, prove such useful tools to those working to determine an accurate diagnosis and plan their treatment or intervention. With different professionals visiting our houses on a regular basis, we inevitably relax on having to scrub the house to the point of immaculate before each visit and allow them to see inside the private world we would normally reserve for friends and family. They see the times when we are down, when things are tough, the days when the smallest step of progress has us disproportionately excited and on top the world, and those days when we are just plain weary.

In addition to the days when we are tired, there can also be black days when it feels like we are trying to move through treacle, when movement forward in a situation is so slow and it takes all our energy to lift one foot and make that next step. We can feel an overwhelming lethargy. So often when our family are in the middle of a situation or crisis, the survival instinct kicks in that enables us to cope and to protect them, and we are able to see that particular crisis through to the end without breaking down. But this just buries the stress, and at some point in the future it is likely to manifest itself in one of these black days. On those days, I have a desire to hide under my duvet and never come out.

One of my toughest times began when Campbell had his cochlear implant operation. Campbell had just turned two and Cameron was three and a half. I went to Manchester with Campbell for his operation and the subsequent three operations that followed over a four-week period to help the area around the implant heal. He and I took up residence in the children's surgical ward for the vast majority of a month. With a couple of weekend passes to visit home and occasional visits from various family members while we were there, it really felt like we had moved in. I had to leave Cameron at home with his dad, who was still working, and his care had to be managed by an assortment of friends and relatives. To look after one child's needs, I had to abandon the other. Whilst I will always be grateful for the support others gave us during that time, I will always feel regret that I had to leave Cameron for that length of time when he, in his own way, still needed me to interpret for him and facilitate his communication with the outside world. It's a symptom of that maternal guilt that arrives on one shoulder, along with the equal amount of responsibility placed on the other shoulder, the minute a newborn is placed in our arms.

In Manchester, things weren't going smoothly following Campbell's first operation, so we were in a cycle of anaesthetics, recovery rooms, needles, X-rays, and head bandages. It was all completely necessary, but my deaf two-year-old could not understand what was happening and I could not adequately prepare him. He was under the microscope, being woken for observations, feeling pain and discomfort, being forced to be still for yet another X-ray, and during that time I had to help with everything and do things no parent ever imagines they will have to do in their child's best interests. Somehow I woke up every day and carried on with a smile on my face and optimism for the next day. There was no other option. Campbell needed me there, needed his mum; one familiar landmark in an otherwise foreign land. As I write this I know our situation is in no way comparable to the medical challenges some parents go through with their children, but I hope others can still relate to my experience.

Campbell finally came home and life went on. His implant was switched on and it was an amazing success, allowing us to rationalise that it had all been worth it. The joy we felt when he turned to sound and when he started to talk, balanced out the bad. My dark time, when I allowed my body and soul to react to what had happened during that period, came a year later, when the cochlear implant team in Manchester suggested that Cameron, then aged four and a half, would also benefit from a cochlear implant. I faced the knowledge that we could go through the same (or better or worse) with Cameron, and that this time it was Campbell I would have to abandon.

It was at that point that my need to hide from the world became too great and I had to give in. I was able to care for the children, but for the time they were in school and in bed of an evening, I hid. Beyond the children's day-to-day welfare, nothing else was important. I couldn't face talking with others about how my children needed yet more intervention or about how things had taken a turn for the worse for us again. I didn't want to explain the deterioration in Cameron's hearing and the implications for me as a parent facing surgery on one of my children again. Most of all, I needed to be alone, to acknowledge to myself how bad that time had been and how it had made me feel, to allow myself to feel the pain. Because just as I had the need to address my stored-up feelings, I then needed to emerge from my duvet, pick myself up, and take the steps forward that needed to be taken: notifying everyone involved with Cameron that this was happening, explaining it to family members, making arrangements for Campbell, and then going through the actual process. Inevitably, the only way is forward, leaving the past and any bad feelings behind and taking with us only positive memories.

Sometimes in this way of life we are getting by, yet events seem to be conspiring against us, and when very little is going well we can easily cross a mental boundary to the dark side. Yoga instructor Tommy Rosen provides a very apt analogy to describe this experience: he says the cycle of negative thoughts we fall into is like a bad neighbourhood in our minds. This image really resonated with me. Imagine: Leaving our usual path with its ups and downs, we cross into this bad neighbourhood where everything works against us and no matter how many side streets we turn down, there seems to be no way out. There's always a dead end with broken or flickering street lights that don't provide adequate illumination for us to see the way out. We pass shops that can't help us right now; they have a long waiting list. Other shops don't think they can help us and suggest a shop further down the block that might be able to help. On the pavements people stand watching us; we feel them judging us as we pass. We sense they think they could find their way better. There are red lights at every junction, delaying us, and detours that seem to take us farther from our destination.

For parents of a child with difficulties, all the little things that commonly occur in our lives quickly build until we can't see past them. The good and positive around us vanishes from view. There is no map to help us navigate out of that bad neighbourhood, and whilst we remain in that negative thought cycle, life is harder. Like any bad neighbourhood, it doesn't influence us in any good way; it merely hardens us and isolates us. Each of us needs to find a bridge back to our regular neighbourhood, and we need to post a sign so that we can recognise the way out of that bad neighbourhood when we need it.

Having friends with whom we can truly relax and appreciate the irony and humour of all our days and situations can also help keep us out of that bad neighbourhood. There is something in these friendships with people who know, who can see it all without being told, which is unspoken but bound by trust. For all of our laughter and fun, we can also recognise those moments when the other needs a break or a gentle shove in the right direction.

It can take time to find other parents with similar experiences. At first, I looked around me and felt like the only one; everyone else seemed to be blessed, without such problems or worries. But eventually I found others, and suddenly I wasn't quite so alone on the path.

Among the first of the other mums I met was Helen. One of the playgroups I went to with the boys when they were little was run by a local church. The boys had been part of their play session from before their diagnosis, and the people there were really supportive of me and the boys once they started wearing hearing aids. At Christmas every year there was a dinner held for all women associated with the church, and as one of the mums from playgroup, I was invited. I knew a lot of the others at the dinner, and I had been seated between a close friend and Helen, who was introduced to me as having recently moved into the area with her two children. Though her family lived such a short walk from our house, we had never met. Our conversation can't have gone more than a couple of sentences before we realised that we had been carefully sat together: her youngest child,

Mikey, was also deaf.

We easily began sharing our experiences. By dessert Helen admitted bashfully in front of the group that Mikey had just ruined a set of hearing aids by dropping them in her cup of tea; she was in the process of getting new ones. 'That's nothing,' said my friend, 'Tamsin has already put one set through the washing machine!' So that kinship was formed before I even had time to admit to the other set of hearing aids that Cameron had flushed down the toilet during our potty-training frenzy! It was such a relief to meet someone who knew what life was like and what could happen, and who could also share my laughter after the event at the absurdity of calling up audiology to admit that, 'Sorry, I put my child's hearing aids, by mistake, through a hot wash! Oops, and could I have some new ones please?!' Sometimes it feels like parts of our lives could lend themselves well to a comedy sketch.

Many years on, I find that my closest friends are very much people who share my way of life. I have other good friends whose company I enjoy and whom I get into all manner of trouble with, but my core group, with whom I find I can laugh, cry, and share my fears, are other mums who at different times feel the way I feel. It is logical that people gravitate towards those on common ground to share challenges, triumphs, and upsets, and within those friendship groupings I found my extended family. Over time and through shared experiences, all of the children in our families, those with difficulties and those without, have become dear to us all. Each small achievement is celebrated by all: my one-and-a-half-year-old goddaughter learning to sign cat (cue everyone finding reasons to point out cats and sign the word with her), my two-year-old showing success at potty training (so everyone does the potty dance), or the revelation that my friend's seven-year-old had for the first time used the word deaf to describe himself when explaining his hearing aids at the doctor's (that one was more of a silent adult celebration, but it tugged all our heart strings equally and made us so proud).

As a group, our families often create chaos. During a recent hot spell, Lisa and I decided that we would put out paddling pools in her garden for our six children to play in while we shared a picnic lunch. Four of the children are deaf and had to remove their equipment before approaching the water. The normal shrieks associated with water play were then multiplied by the fact that the children couldn't communicate with the others easily, couldn't get their attention, and, most importantly, couldn't get them to stop the hose! The noise level was off the charts. But the children had a blast, and so did we, watching and occasionally being splashed. The children felt free just to enjoy themselves and we laughed nonstop. I'm sure it wasn't the most peaceful afternoon for the neighbours, but we promise not to do it again until the next hot spell!

Parents like us often don't feel we have the freedom to allow our children to enjoy themselves if we're in a public place or out with families whose children don't have difficulties. If the children are at the swimming pool and don't respond because they don't have their equipment on, or ignore us at the park because they have gone slightly too far away and don't hear our call, we can often feel people's eyes, both real and imaginary, on us. We feel like they must be thinking we can't control our children. That bad neighbourhood I described earlier is only a few streets away in our minds, and we become uptight as we try to ensure that our children are behaving to a standard that no one can question – but in doing so we stifle them.

It's easy to slip into the paranoia that people are judging us because our children are loud or seemingly disruptive. In some cases, this paranoia is just that: paranoia. It is based on nothing but our own insecurity, and it is unfair on those we transfer the feelings onto. However, in other cases, it is rooted in past experiences where people expressed their displeasure at the noise the children made or passed comment on how they would approach the children's behaviour. As parents we can be torn between conflicting feelings of wanting to explain and soothe the situation and feeling angry that people feel they have the right to judge without knowing the whole story.

I remember interviewing a mum of a young child with autism when I was student, long before I had my own children. I was talking to her to gain background information for a project I had to complete as part of my placement, and her honesty struck me and has stayed with me. When I asked her about her daily life with her son, she explained that some days she couldn't face going out their front door with him for the looks and glares and comments she felt she might receive. Some days she felt the energy to deal with them, and on others it was beyond her. She recalled a day when she had taken her son to the local butchers. Unfortunately, they were unable to buy his favourite sausages that were part of his routine every time they visited that shop. Her son could not cope with this break in routine and began to lash out verbally and physically at himself and his mother. His mum remembered feeling ashamed that he was causing a scene and hearing the murmurs and comments from people behind her in the queue, and also feeling in equal measure the need to protect her son from people who didn't understand him. She walked out of the shop without her groceries and didn't look back. Instances like this made her feel so inhibited about taking her son out that she started to avoid it, further isolating them. To avoid those feelings is difficult and takes a conscious effort. These situations lead us to treasure even more those times when we can relax with friends without needing to justify or explain anything to ourselves or others.

Part of our way of life is educating others about it. This carries its own difficulties, but having done so I can say the results can be amazing. When Campbell was eight years old, we realised that he was coping superbly well within the mainstream class without needing support from the hearing resource base and was progressing with great strides educationally. However, his grouping with his deaf peers was now working against him. Because of the severity of his hearing loss, he had not learned the valuable social rules and nuances that toddlers usually pick up in their very early interactions with their peers at playgroups and such. Later, for class activities and during play time at school, he was often paired with another boy his age who also had a cochlear implant. This meant that at the age of eight he found it hard to cope in small friendship groups with his hearing peers. He wasn't familiar with all the nuances of early friendships that we remember well from our own childhood; he didn't know that he could have a disagreement with a friend and still be friends with him the next day. The situation was upsetting him and having a dramatic effect on his behaviour at home. We eventually made the decision that it would be wise to explore the option for Campbell to attend our local mainstream school, where he could access more out-of-school clubs and have friends home to play more easily. It would also separate our boys; they were close in age and had naturally been grouped together over the years, and we thought this would give them an opportunity to grow a bit more into their identities as individuals.

When I first left a message for the head teacher of our local school, I did so knowing they had previously had deaf children in the school and having heard good reports from other parents that it was a school that wanted the best for their pupils. It had taken a lot to get to the point of making this approach, and I was therefore stunned when the head teacher returned my call and almost immediately told me that her school could not meet Campbell's needs. I struggled to respond. She hadn't met Campbell, and hadn't heard from me why we were approaching them, so why would she push him away? The answer, I thought, was fear. The school mentioned that although they had previously had deaf pupils, they had never had a student with a cochlear implant. This initial conversation left me feeling that to the outside world my son was a freak of some sort, a boy with two heads who was potentially too big a burden for anyone to take on. My initial reaction was of shock and anger; I did not want to have anything to do with a school that could make me feel that way and be so misinformed as to not be willing to give my son a chance.

I turned to the head of our local Sensory Service, which supports deaf children in mainstream school as appropriate. He had initially been very encouraging about our investigating this move for Campbell; he felt it was an appropriate and positive step. When I spoke to him he acknowledged my feelings and knew that behind my anger I was hurting, yet whilst calming me he also planted the seed that if this was the right decision for Campbell, and we had already come this far, maybe some persistence and education would provide the outcome we hoped for. For a while I couldn't face the idea of contacting the school again; my anger was too great. But slowly, the seed that had been planted germinated, and I decided that this was yet another thing in the boys' lives that was worth fighting for. I contacted the school and asked if we could arrange a visit for Lee and I (despite our divorce we still jointly consider these decisions) to see the school and discuss their inhibitions to having Campbell as a student. If this went well, we would then take Campbell to visit the school so they could see and hear him in the flesh – exhibit A, if you like. They agreed.

When we visited the school, we were impressed with what we saw on our tour. Then came the time to hear their fears: could they meet his educational needs? We showed them copies of his reports, and this was easily answered in the affirmative. They had no experience with the equipment; how could they fix it if it broke? This one was also easily met: I lived a few streets away and was more than happy to come up and troubleshoot difficulties and work with them if necessary; there was also training which could be provided for them. They were a large school and expressed concern for the possibly devastating consequences if he were to fall in their playground and bang his head (for a child with a cochlear implant, a bang to the head could displace the internal component, which would then need to be removed, with no guarantee that it could be re-implanted later). This is where educating them about our way of life came in. I explained that we live our life with the knowledge that the children could trip over their own feet getting out of bed and bang their head, or they could slip in the shower and do the same. There are numerous other possible scenarios, and all of them and more could happen before we even leave our house in the morning. There are certain things we can take logical precautions against – for example, the boys will never be able to bungee jump (one less thing for their mother to worry about!), because this too could displace the internal component. A few other activities, such as martial arts, are advised against for the risks they pose to the implant, but beyond that the boys cannot let any of this stop them from living.

After our conversation, the head teacher seemed reassured and more confident in the school's ability to cope with a student like Campbell. Her fears of the unknown lessened, and she felt comfortable that we only had realistic expectations of them. Campbell went to visit, and the following school year he started there. The school have been fantastic. There have been learning moments, such as the day they went on a class trip and forgot to take spare batteries with them; Campbell spent most of the day in silence and had to stand beside the teacher who frantically wrote things out for him, desperate that he not miss out. It won't happen again, and if it did I know they would feel just as bad about it as I do. I am now able to walk Campbell to school and collect him, and this time is so valuable for him to share his thoughts and ideas from the day. He goes to the school he knows his younger sister will soon attend, and in a few months he will be going with his class on a week's trip to France. It is going to be a long, hard journey over the next few years for Campbell socially, but he recently had a friend for a sleepover for the first time and the night was a success; this gives me confidence that we are on the right road for him. I could so easily have walked away from the fight to have him change schools, but I am so glad I had a friendly voice to encourage me to give it another try.

Butterfly

Life is not about waiting for the storm to pass. It is about learning to dance in the rain.
– Anonymous

I have learned that to be with those I like is enough
– Walt Whitman

In early February 2009 I was in the latter stages of planning my wedding to my second husband. I was going through the blooming stage of pregnancy with my third child due that summer, and the boys were then eight and six. The planning passed in a haze of much-needed organisation from my oldest friend, Janine. She is an expert in event planning and soon gathered that I seemed to have a notion for anything on the butterfly theme. We spent hours scouring the internet, shops, and catalogues until the wedding had a definite butterfly stamp on it, from the jewellery to centrepieces to the stunning wedding cake my future mother-in-law created for us. The theme became so prominent that my mother commented to me during the reception that she had never realised I had such an affinity for butterfly imagery. It wasn't something I had thought about consciously, and I couldn't explain it, but the butterflies did have meaning for me.

From then on I have become more aware of my attraction to the butterfly's beauty and symbolism. The butterfly's wings convey fragility in their structure, graceful silhouette, and intricate patterns. The butterfly is a creature that is able to enjoy the sunniest of days, that seemingly floats within our vision to draw our attention to the flowers and plants we could so easily walk past. Each butterfly is so unique and sure in its movements.

I have often wondered at this creature and its significance to me, and as usual my first port of call was Google, where I found many variations on the theme of the butterfly and its meaning. The one that spoke most to me compared the human experience to the butterfly's transformation process. In the beginning of life, we are all small and appear the same, like the caterpillar. As we grow older and change with life events our true beauty shows, like the butterfly's. Just like butterflies, we are all different and beautiful in our own way, each with our own special mix of strengths and weaknesses and unique character.

Reflecting further, I realised how true this is: We all start out pretty much the same as nappy-wearing, milk-drinking babies. For some, the life lessons that make each of us unique begin during these early stages. Most of us will then go through similar rites of passage such as education, sibling rivalry, friendships, and early relationships. We then reach a stage of early adulthood where all the paths multiply tenfold and diverge, and we're shaped by the path we choose and the unique experiences it leads us to. For me, life seemed so clearly mapped and uniform: engagement, marriage, house, move for work, couples nights, planning a family. Then my children arrived and we entered uncharted territory. I was constantly learning, shifting with the terrain, and beginning to understand myself, what drove me, and what I needed to sustain me in this section of my life. To provide all that my children needed, so much of which was not material, I had to find the unique balance that would fulfil me as an individual. Then I emerged from this chrysalis, ready to marry for a second time, embarking on a shared path again, confident in my choices and my ability to express my needs, complementing the 'yin' value Matt adds to my 'yang'.

By this stage in my life I had learned and come to understand a lot about who I am. The woman I saw in the mirror every morning had grown so much; although often stressed and harassed looking, she seemed to have an inner confidence in herself and her capabilities and a ready smile for her children's absurd antics. I could recognise some aspects as being the same as they were ten years earlier, those essential parts of my character that are innate, like my over-enthusiastic optimism in situations, which I'm sure my husband wishes would develop a tiny leak; a genuine interest in others and their lives and stories, coupled with a desire to help and facilitate as much as I can. Other aspects I saw were less familiar. I have changed over the years I've been a parent to my children; over time one cannot help but transform through knowledge and experience.

I now see in myself a person who is harder in parts than she had been before. This is a by-product of learning that I need to fight and stand up for my children because I am the only one who will. I have to face people and remind myself that how they feel about me following our interaction is not as important as the outcome for my children. It is not something I have found easy – at heart, I am a people pleaser – but I'm motivated purely by the needs of my children.

My priorities are so different to those of many other parents. I have become dismissive of minor problems and difficulties I see them struggling with, but I can still pull myself back to view them more compassionately when I remind myself to do so. We all worry about major things such as the health or safety of our families, but I don't berate myself if, in a bad week of appointments when our family is in chaos, the children have consecutive nights of junk food and ice cream. I value my children having a healthy diet and expose them to a variety of tastes, but I'm able to balance the good I generally achieve in this area with the concessions I need to make in times of stress. On those crazy days, sanity is worth more than the five-a-day rule.

I try to stay focussed in order to finish all the tasks having to do with my children and running a family, but I find there is never an end to the ironing pile and there is always dust thick enough to write in somewhere in the house. But I don't apologise! Something that years ago I would have felt I needed to make excuses for and would have felt was a failing, I now accept as collateral damage. With the myriad of tasks that forms my to-do lists, there will never be enough hours in the day to cross off every item. Amidst the costumes needed for a '60s day at school, the appointment to collect a new hearing aid and mould, library books to be returned, a school meeting about support levels, and daily cooking and cleaning, to name just a few, there will be things which get missed or put to the top of tomorrow's list. However, the missing football kit, which is still absent as I write this, is fast approaching emergency status!

In mentioning all the chores and appointments that prevent me from completing everything there is to do, I have omitted another important reason why my objectives get delayed: spontaneity. When I was younger I felt driven to complete tasks meticulously, to the detriment of any opportunities which arose in the meantime. Now I treasure brief or extended times in my day for the pure enjoyment of a moment (the minutiae can wait for later). When summer chooses to arrive, the first place we head to is the park to enjoy the warmth of the sun on our skin, allowing the children to run in the fresh air and play hide-and-seek amongst the trees. These simple pleasures are so enjoyable and it's important to take advantage of these opportunities when they present themselves. Who knows if we will be able to enjoy the outdoors the next time the sun is out; I could well be inside a hospital waiting room containing the children's frustration whilst we wait to be seen for an appointment. Spontaneous moments are so fulfilling and enriching, and I am so glad my children have taught me to recognise the possibilities they hold and to abandon control of my schedule to allow for them. This is where I find the balance in my life. Happy moments with my children are the light which takes away the shade. I suppose the shade is necessary in life for us to truly appreciate the rays of light that come to banish it, but I must admit I am partial to those light moments.

One major area has taken me longer to accept and unravel: I have depended on my own ever-increasing independence and self-sufficiency to fulfil my role as mum to my boys. The bottom line is that I am the person who needs to do this. To me there has been no other option, and to achieve all that needs to be done I have relied on myself and my inner strength. This has in turn been empowering and positive in my personal growth and self-esteem; whatever obstacle comes next, I believe we will see it through and move forward positively, if slightly ruffled around the edges from the episode.

The more negative aspect this approach has had on my character is that I find it a challenge to rely on those around me. Once, during a conversation with another parent, as we discussed some of our more trying times, she commented to me, 'You don't ever seem to need help'. What she said made me pause, and I explained that this wasn't the case. I frequently feel the need for support, for someone to remove the weight from my shoulders, if only for a second, so I can breathe and recoup my strength. I could see now, though, that this wasn't the image I portrayed to the world at large. Mine was an image of someone in control, sure of themselves, and not in need of outside help. In expecting to meet all of my children's needs myself, I had created a place that did not invite others to doubt my capability, but which was not necessarily a true reflection of my inner feelings.

Since that conversation I have become ever more conscious of how I represent myself in times of need, those portions of our trek when I'm busy but just about coping and also those when I really could use some help to surmount our latest hurdle – when I'm not so much Super Woman but more like Road Runner, racing from place to place at a frantic pace, acknowledging I will probably miss something on my way past. And here's the biggie that my new husband has been helping me with: learning to trust that someone other than me is capable of going back to pick up those bits I've missed, that I don't have to do that too. I'm learning that I can pass over some of the load that I have been so conscious of not putting onto others for fear of being let down, of overextending the imaginary bounds of friendship, and of 'putting upon' people.

I am not the only one who has had to adapt and evolve in order to survive and to help my family thrive in the different environments we inhabit. Plenty of other people are also seeking their own identity and niche in their world, as the parent of a child who has more challenges. All families will parent in their own way, nurturing, supporting, and helping their children flourish. Parents' approaches to parenting do not change completely because of the experiences they have been through with a child who has difficulties. Their approach is also informed by their own childhoods, values, and morals. We don't all become identical families; there's not a Stepford wife in sight. There exists, however, a kinship between parents who have shared experiences that makes it easy for us to relate to each other and become comfortable in each other's presence. I have seen and been part of this in so many ways: bonding on hospital wards where the parents help each other out with the routines in place, sharing responsibility for each other's children to allow for shower breaks, and carry out sneaky raids to acquire extra linen when needed; phone calls for support and discussions over important decisions that would not be the same with another adult friend; it is a fascinating cooperative and mutually beneficial bond, an unbelievable support system.

It is natural, then, that those of us who have changed because of our journey, gravitate towards people who have had similar experiences and who are aware of our way of life. This does not mean that my only friends are those whose children have needs that are similar to my children's, though. I have a fantastic group of friends who have helped me sample the delights of comedy nights, burlesque, and numerous other adventures during my rare nights out. They help me remember that I still have my own identity and that I am not only someone's mum. Nevertheless, when I am feeling more pressured about the children, it is with other parents like me that I am often most comfortable.

As parents of children with difficulties we learn to accept that we cannot control many parts of our lives. Any broken equipment, fluctuations in hearing loss and increasing levels of need in our children are beyond our power. We can, however, influence our environment. We can take our experiences and acquired knowledge and be empowered as individuals, and as part of a group, to believe in our own point of view and share it. As parents we will always know our child best. Not in a blinkered and unreceptive way, but in a way that recognises all those little indicators a child uses to show how he or she is feeling and coping. These can only be learned by comforting our children from small grazes and big fears, in celebrating their achievements, and seeing the growing confidence and joy reflected in their eyes and smiles.

I have learned never to be frightened to share my instincts about my children when in health appointments or educational reviews. This hasn't been an easy feat for the girl who spent her time in school doing her best to blend in. I may review my opinion once others share their views, but the fact remains that no one else will be looking at my child and his situation from my unique vantage point. Many, many reviews down the road, I have accepted that I am the only person who can say these things and add these vital points. It may not make me the most popular parent in some situations, but I know that in the future I won't look back and regret the fear that kept me from speaking up. I'll know that I have done all that is within my power for my children and their development.

It can often be more comfortable to work together as a group in order to influence change for our children. In our area we were recently faced with a possible reduction in specialist educational support for hearing impaired and deaf children within their individual schools. This support is vital to the children's success in school and how confident they feel within their classroom setting.

Every child receives a differing level of this support based on age, needs, and progress. Numerous families came together, from those whose children received no support through to families whose children depended on much higher levels of support. There were parents of children with mild hearing loss as well as those of children with profound loss, all there to express as a collective that our children would not cope if the possible reduction became a reality. Our united voice was heard and that proposed change did not happen; for now the provision has been preserved, and we feel such relief and satisfaction in this result.

Now, I'm inspired by empowering people to see the difference they can make and the crucial role they play in their child's life and progress. In 2011, I met a family who was caring for a little boy with a cochlear implant. They had lost sight of the value they brought to his life and felt that they were failing him. Our meeting was by chance; whilst we were both attending routine reviews at the implant centre we met in the waiting room and later outside. While we talked our children engaged in an impromptu game of chase; soon giggles were heard and the fun they were having was evident. The lady I was chatting with turned to this sound, and it was only as she smiled that I recognised the strain she'd exhibited during the rest of our conversation. She was weighed down with concern and worry and it was draining her. Both she and her partner were committed to doing the best they could for the little boy, but they were currently experiencing lots of negative comments regarding his progress. 'He should be doing better', the experts said, 'There should have been more marked progress over the past couple of months.'

Yet, because of the child's difficult family situation they had been focussing more on keeping his life as stable as possible and providing him with a loving, reassuring, and constant environment. There was no doubt they were succeeding in this regard. The little boy playing beside us was happy, calm, and enjoying himself in a simple game with others without adult involvement. Although the couple were aware of his language targets, while they had been focussed on getting him settled he had not made as much progress with verbal and listening skills as the professionals would have liked. This could be for a variety of reasons, but his carers felt the professionals had placed the emphasis on them for failing him, suggesting they were not doing enough for him. In dealing with these thoughts and the associated guilt and blame, they were finding it harder to tap into their reserves to keep going. They needed to continue to do what was working and hopefully amplify progress on other targets, perhaps by being creative with other ways they could encourage listening and language.

They felt so unsure of their skills and ability to follow through that they were prepared to share their feelings with me, a stranger. My advice was simple: 'Keep doing what you are doing, because you are doing a good job, and everything else will follow in time'. She responded with surprised relief and an acknowledgement that because the focus of attention had been on the negatives so much recently, they had become ground down and unable to see a positive in what they were doing. I didn't offer them a solution or a magic answer (there isn't one), but instead tried to fortify them to continue. I had been lucky enough to have people say those same words to me in the past and it helped me keep trying, to keep moving forward even if at a slow pace, and to keep having faith that continued effort and consistency would in time reap the rewards we hoped for.

Being parents or carers to children with difficulties means often having to lay out normally private family details for professionals to glance over and dissect. This vulnerable experience is so often repeated that it is only natural that we can find some of our self-worth becoming dependant on the approval of these outside people. They are measuring and observing our children, but as we have so much invested emotionally in the outcome, their observations are intertwined with an assessment of our parenting. We want them to be happy with the progress we have helped our child achieve and praise the techniques we are using, but often if we receive no feedback or there is concern noted, it can start that niggle of doubt. The professional most probably is unaware of the impact that her comments can have. This can also be compounded by friends or family members who pass an innocent comment over what they have heard or seen. Again, if we do not have confidence in ourselves and self-belief that we are doing a good job as parents, these comments can make us feel judged and dragged down by the implication that we aren't good enough.

To all children, at the most basic level, their parents will always be good enough; they are irreplaceable people in their lives. We can use this as a foundation to build from. We have to believe in ourselves as they do and believe that as long as we are trying our best, learning and adapting as we go, then we are being the best parents we can be. None of us will ever be the perfect parent all the time. We will all have moments where we can look back and think 'Ooops!' or 'Next time we'll do that differently' whilst we clean up the subsequent mess or soothe and reassure frayed tempers and hurt feelings. However, when we don't value ourselves and what we contribute daily to our children, we give away a vital element of the strength we need to continue – day in, day out.

Through all I have written I have focussed on the stages I have transitioned through as a parent. Another key component in finding the resources from within to sustain me on this journey has been, as I mentioned earlier, remembering that I have an identity which is independent of my role as a mum – not in any way to deny my parental responsibilities, but instead to achieve an inner harmony.

One of my favourite quotes is 'A wise woman waters her own garden first'. It is something I have to remind myself of often, and when time and energy allow I get out my metaphorical watering can. In the initial phase of being a mum and then the chaos following the boys' diagnosis, I got by as well as I could. All my energy poured into my children. Then someone reminded me that there was still a 'me' who was independent of the role I fulfilled for my children. An essential part of me had been buried for a while, but I would need to find it again in order to continue to progress. The rediscovering of that 'me' has taken time and has been influenced by all the changes I have noted so far.

Over the past five years I have learned what I need to nourish myself. I wish for excitement's sake I could tell you it takes the form of some dramatic and exotic hobby such as crocodile wrestling, belly dancing, or high-wire gymnastics, but in reality it is much more mundane. I lose myself in characters other authors develop in books, and I become gripped by the tales they weave. I have also become the queen of the DVD box set. I have discovered series that I can watch back to back, snuggled up under my duvet, when I need to hide from and tune out the world. I immerse myself in landscapes and storylines that feature terrorist threats and double agents, but bear no relation on my life. I have found the religion of Jack Bauer. I have also remembered to indulge my dry sense of humour. Comedy nights and good friends who share my sense of irony have led to times when my sides ache from laughing. Running has given me space and time to think, to contemplate life and work it out as I cover mile after mile. Organising events and fundraising for our local deaf children's group, brings unique fulfilment to my life by enabling children to interact with others they can identify with and bringing their families together. All these activities help me pour out stress and rebuild strength to face each new day and whatever it brings. All come together to form the butterfly I have become.

Recently we took a trip to Scotland to attend a family friend's wedding. Once we crossed the border and drew closer to my home city of Edinburgh, everything we passed became more and more familiar to me. Reminiscences, thoughts, and feelings from my time in this city came flooding back. A song from my teenage years began to play silently in my head: 'Caledonia you're calling me and now I'm going home'. The depth of the roots stirring within surprised me after my time away. As we drove through areas of Edinburgh where I had spent time as a student, I remembered all my notions from that time as to what my future would be like. I had walked these streets, believing I would always live here and raise my family within sight of landmarks I had known all my life. I had so many scenarios of how my life would play out, as everyone does as they grow into adulthood and imagine their future. As I looked out the car window I was aware that my life now barely resembles those images I had once held in my head. All the thoughts and nostalgia were overwhelming, but an unshakeable truth also emerged: my life is elsewhere now. This was a holiday and not where I belong. I belong in my own life, where everything is as it should be. There's no point in wondering 'what if?' My life is richer for the challenges and worries we have faced. Without them I wouldn't be the mother I am today, the woman I am today. I would not have had all of the experiences, moments, interactions, and friendships which I treasure.

So here is where this story ends for now. Orson Welles said, 'If you want a happy ending, that depends, of course, on where you stop your story'. This travel journal of my trek as a parent is not complete, but this is a natural point at which to close, and it is definitely our version of a happy ending. We are still on our journey as a family, with many new challenges to face, I'm sure, and more lessons for me to learn as a parent. There will be days when an overwhelming sense of worries, guilt, and responsibilities will resurface and my focus will narrow to merely getting through each day with all those I care about safe and sound. The rest will wait for a day, at least. We are a family with direction but with our eyes on the present, taking as much from each minute as we can. Smiling and laughing as we go.

Around the corner, tomorrow, next week... Our lives will change with each new event, appointment, situation or result. But until we get there, we'll do what we've always done and meanwhile, keep dancing.

Further Information

Hearing Loss and Cochlear Implants

- Not all people with a hearing loss wear a hearing aid, cochlear implant, or other type of technology to aid their hearing. This can be for a variety of reasons, but it does not mean they don't struggle with hearing the world around them.

- Hearing loss is described as either conductive or sensorineural.

- Conductive hearing loss describes a hearing loss which occurs when sound cannot move freely from the outer ear through to the inner ear. One of the most common causes of this type of hearing loss is fluid build-up in the middle ear, which prevents sound from being transmitted effectively in the usual way. Most types of conductive loss can be treated, so it is considered more of a 'temporary' loss. A conductive hearing loss can occur in isolation or in conjunction with a sensorineural loss.

- Sensorineural hearing loss manifests when there is damage to the structure of the inner ear or to the nerve pathways which lead from the inner ear to the brain. It most often occurs when there is damage or absence of the hair cells. The causes of this type of hearing loss vary widely and include genetic causes, head trauma, exposure to loud noises, illnesses such as measles and meningitis, or even side effects of medication used to treat another medical condition. The majority of this type of hearing loss cannot be corrected by medical or surgical treatment. Sensorineural loss is the most common type of permanent hearing loss and can cause a mild, moderate, severe, or profound level of loss.

- Hearing loss can occur in both of a person's ears or in just one. Hearing loss in both ears is called bilateral loss, and loss in just one ear is called a unilateral loss. If there is hearing loss in both ears, the level of loss can differ between the ears, with more extensive hearing loss in one ear than the other.

- In some types of hearing loss the degree of difficulty in hearing can fluctuate;

at times the person's hearing can be worse than at others. For some people these periods can be triggered by various factors, but for other people it can be completely random. An established hearing loss can also be increased by fluid in the ear canal from a cold or virus, creating an additional conductive hearing loss.

- In some cases hearing loss can be progressive. For many people their hearing loss will stay the same from diagnosis onwards, but for others it can deteriorate over time. This deterioration can be swift or be spread gradually over years. It can also be affected by head trauma or other factors, such as the air pressure one encounters when diving or flying. Progressive hearing loss can cause confusion in the diagnosis and assessment process; hearing which appeared normal at one testing can change over the following months to such a degree that it causes significant difficulty for the individual.

- I focus here on the specific technology of hearing aids and cochlear implants, but there is a huge range of specialist equipment that is used to help those with hearing difficulties, such as bone-anchored hearing aids and many others. There is constant research to explore new ways to help people hear. Some of the latest developments are middle-ear implants and trials of cochlear implants where all of the implant is located under the skin, with no exterior components. It is worth fully exploring this constantly changing landscape and keeping up-to-date with all developments.

Cochlea or Cochlear

It is worth noting that the word 'cochlea' describes part of the inner ear whilst 'cochlear (implant)' is the name of the device.

Terminology

Unfamiliar terms and words often appear in reports on hearing assessments and in conversations with professionals. Parents may be unsure of their meaning and the implications they have for their child, but they may not wish to admit that they don't know what they mean. Here are some of the words they may encounter.

Chronological age: This is a child's age at the time of testing. This might be described, for example, as '2 years, 10 months' or '2;10 years'.

Age equivalent: This is the age that a test has assessed as a child's current level of development in one area. This may be younger than the child's actual age, so a child could be 3 years, 6 months but have an age equivalent of 2 years, 6 months. A child may have different age equivalents for different areas of development. The age equivalent for motor development (walking, etc.), for example, may be the same as the child's chronological age, but communication development could be similar to that of a child who is a year younger, indicating a delay compared to the rest of the child's skills.

Hearing age: This is a term used to describe how long a child with a hearing loss has had hearing aids or a cochlear implant to aid hearing. If a child was given a cochlear implant at age one, when he is six years old he would be described as having a hearing age of five.

Receptive language: This is a term used to describe what spoken language a child can understand. It may, at times, also be assessed separately as the sign language a child can understand. This assessment tries to gauge how much a child can understand without the subtle clues of everyday life that provide 'situation understanding', such as when the speaker points with his eyes, moves his head towards the object asked for, or holds a bag and car keys whilst telling the child to get her shoes. These cues can hide some of the difficulties a child may be having in understanding language.

Expressive language: This is a term used to describe the language a child uses to express herself and her wants and needs. This can encompass the spoken sounds or words she uses as well as the signs or gestures she may use to communicate with those around her. As the child becomes a more skilled communicator and her use of expressive language increases, more areas are discussed under this heading. It is broken down into the amount of information the child tells us with what she says, the vocabulary she includes, and the grammar she has learned to use. Breaking down a child's communication into these groups can help the people working with her focus on areas that need improvement.

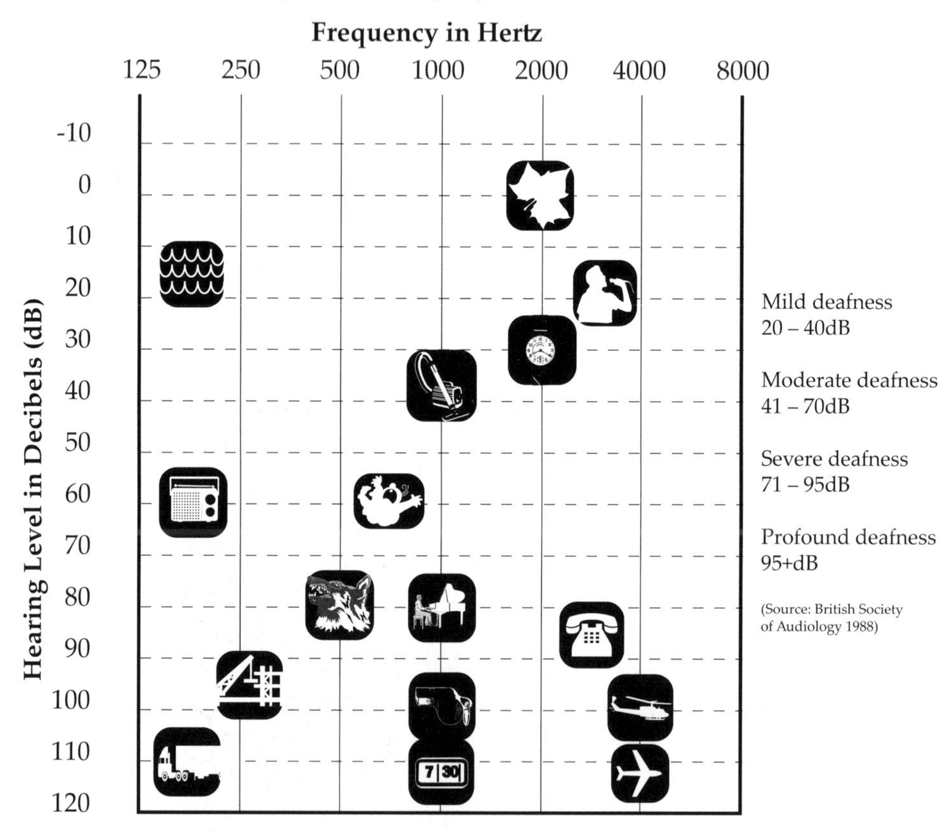
A visual representation of the loudness and pitch of everyday sounds
Frequency in Hertz
125
250
500
1000
2000
4000
8000
Hearing Level in Decibels (dB)
-10
0
10
20
30
40
50
60
70
80
90
100
110
120
7|30
Mild deafness
20 – 40dB
Moderate deafness
41 – 70dB
Severe deafness
71 – 95dB
Profound deafness
95+dB
(Source: British Society of Audiology 1988)

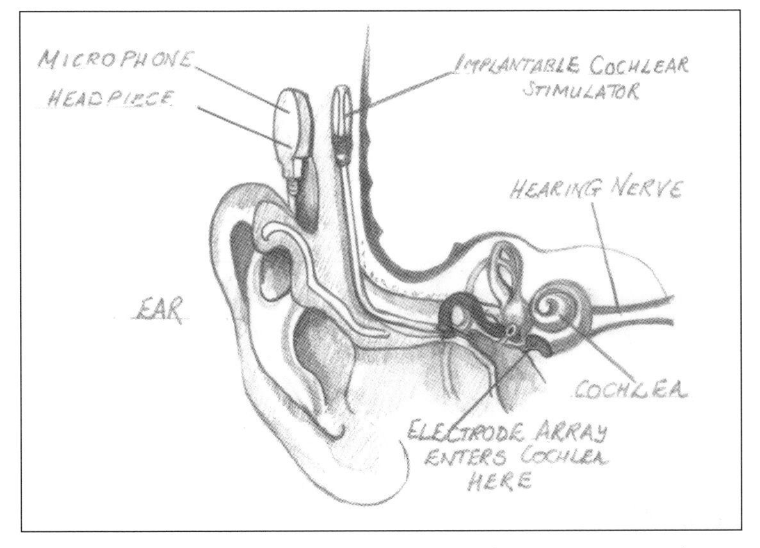

An artist's representation of how cochlear implants are currently inserted

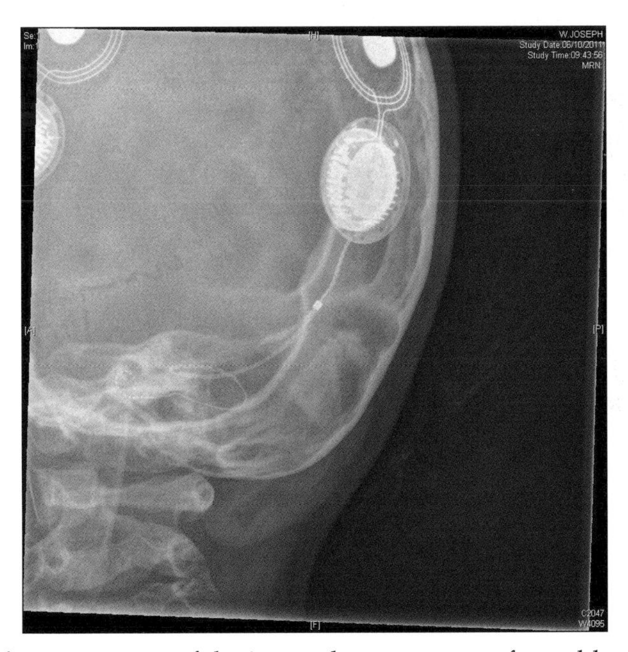

An x-ray of the positioning of the internal components of a cochlear implant, in a four year old. This x-ray is of a little boy who had a second implant inserted at the age of 4 years. In the top left hand corner of the picture you can see the original implant on the left hand side of his head also. Thank you to Joseph and his mummy Claire for letting us show this image.

Other Information Resources

At the time my boys were diagnosed, access to information sources through the internet was in its' infancy. Since then the diversity of information available through the web and the ability to reach out to other people through social media has blossomed, flourished and downright taken over! There are now websites, forums, blogs, Face book and Twitter resources that families can search through and whilst some will fit better for individual families than others it is worth a look. Where parents before have felt isolated by geographical distance from other families who have similar situations to them, or are still not ready to meet others yet in person, there is now the ability to reach out and connect with other families through your mobile or computer screens.

I have found I can keep in contact with many of my friends who are also parents of deaf children, who live in our area and those who have moved further afield, easily using Facebook and Twitter. Through use of social media we can share small steps of progress, triumphs and frustrations with the click of a few keys. We can share pictures and spread new information and developments easily.

The National Deaf Children's Society (NDCS) have a group on face book where parents can post questions or comments and the other members of the group come together as a community to answer any queries or requests for advice they have. Among these groups people also post about exciting developments such as the recent stocking of plush hearing aids in the Build a Bear stores in the UK now!! Trivial to some but for others an accessory their child will love to make their teddy match them.

A lot of the local NDCS groups also have their own face book groups, which families can join, where upcoming events for deaf children and their families and local issues are advertised.

In addition to its formal website (www.ndcs.org.uk) NDCS also runs a helpline during office hours which you can phone for advice and help. Through the helpline you can also register to receive their regular news magazine and information about the events they provide for deaf children and their families or request some help from their local family officer. The helpline number is 0808 800 8880.

The following organisations also have websites; The Ear Foundation (www. earfoundation.org.uk), Action on Hearing Loss (www.actiononhearingloss.org.

uk) where families can find details of courses they run, products they can supply, parent forums and information pages.

A website our family has found useful is Limping Chicken, which was launched in 2012, (www.limpingchicken.co.uk). It is a website which offers new articles every weekday which include news, features and opinion on deaf issues and culture in the UK! This site is well worth a visit as it presents relevant news and interesting articles in an easy to read format. They also have all their old articles archived on the site. There is an option to receive their newsletters direct to your e-mail address.

Amongst the information on the internet there have, in recent years, been more resources which have become available that families may find useful for raising deaf awareness within their family, with siblings, in school, or to encourage their child to wear their hearing aids or implants. Online book stockists we have used include; Action Deafness Books (www.actiondeafnessbooks.org.uk), Forest Books (www.forestbooks.com) and Amazon.

Books that our family has found particularly useful have been 'Freddie and the Fairy' by Julia Donaldson and 'My Brother John' and 'John gets ready for school' by Joanne Zellweger. In addition there are now accessories which families I know have used on hearing aids, such as 'tube riders' to decorate the hearing aids, which have encouraged children to wear them with pride and confidence. For children with cochlear implants, some of the newer implants can be fitted with funky 'sleeves' which give the children the opportunity to express their individuality. It is different for each implant and implant manufacturer, but it is worth looking into your particular provider to check for possibilities.

A Final Message

Someone once told me that when they looked into my eyes they felt like a better person. In my face they had seen a reflection of all the goodness that others could see in them and their actions, but that had become hidden from their own view by the tarnish of day-to-day life, leaving only a lacklustre image in its place.

That is why I wrote this book: to provide a mirror for any parents who feel like their family is going through something alone, bearing the equally heavy burdens of responsibility and parental guilt, both deserved and undeserved. I want to reflect back that they are not alone on their journey and that they are stronger and more capable than they think they are.

This is my message: try to put that stick you are beating yourself up with back in the closet and use that energy to move forward! You are better at what you are doing and achieving than you think you are. Remember and take pride in all the small things. Take belief that whatever you accomplish today is enough and you are sufficient, you are not lacking. To think that will only pull you back and create resistance to your progress onwards. There will always be a voice of doubt, questioning your decisions, your abilities, and your capability – be it from outside or within. Try to quieten it with the noises of your children, their giggles, their laughter, their sounds… for they are the true value in your life.

If one parent can pick up this book and learn appreciation for what he does; gain strength from recognising that he is part of a larger culture of people out there, often isolated but definitely not alone; and face the next hurdle in life while enjoying the simple day-to-day joys, then it has served its purpose. I hope this book gives comfort and understanding to more than one parent or family. To anyone else who picks up this book… thank you for reading it.

I know that my story will resonate with others as being similar or very different to their own experiences. I invite everyone to come and share their experiences and stories at www.afriendlyear.com, a website created to build a community of parents who can share, advise and inspire each other. Come join us!

actionDEAFNESSBooks

Innovative and progressive, Action Deafness Books is the UK's leading publisher and online retailer of books on D/deafness and D/deaf issues.

By D/deaf people, for D/deaf and hearing alike, Action Deafness Books works to deliver a publishing platform that enables people to put their experiences and writing into the public domain. To empower D/deaf people to write, to record and use language – at the same time, allowing hearing people to learn of the D/deaf experience through the works we publish.

But what is more, we work to promote and foster integration between D/deaf and Hearing publishers, distributors and booksellers; to bring the two worlds together in a unique association of interests and one that facilitates learning, the development of new ideas and the sharing of best practice.

We're hugely excited with our success to date - we've worked with the likes of Jacqueline Wilson, Julia Donaldson and Joyce Dunbar; we've published new writing by authors such as Nick Sturley, Tamsin Coates, Ken Carter and Dr. Harold Silver. Our U Sign brand has become an instant hit and we've commissioned a range of children's adventure books – all of which feature D/deaf children as heroes!

From the London Book Fair to the Leicester Literary Festival, the Library Show to the DocWoof Film Festival, we've engendered D/deaf awareness and allowed D/deaf people to be full and participant members of the literary world!

It's an exciting journey we're on and we want you to be part of it! If you are a D/deaf, hard of hearing, deafened or deafblind author with existing work in print or if you aspire to be a published author, then do get in touch – we want to hear from you!

Contact us at: adbooks@actiondeafness.org.uk

Visit: www.actiondeafnessbooks.org.uk

Follow us on Twitter @ActionDeafBooks